CW00493191

A Catalogue of the Cobbe Collection of Keyboard Instruments with Composer Associations

COMPOSER INSTRUMENTS

A CATALOGUE OF THE COBBE COLLECTION OF KEYBOARD INSTRUMENTS WITH COMPOSER ASSOCIATIONS

by Alec Cobbe

Technical Data compiled by David Hunt

THE COBBE COLLECTION TRUST IN ASSOCIATION WITH THE NATIONAL TRUST
2000

To my wife Isabel, who was once told by a fortune-teller that the man she would marry would surround her with music, and to my friend Donald Kahn whose musical insight and generous enthusiasm has given these instruments their future.

Front cover: The keyboard of Mahler's piano (No 28) made by Conrad Graf, with a photograph of Mahler and an autograph fragment of his Tenth Symphony on the music desk.

Back cover: Front panel of King Charles II virginals (No. 4) showing the WP brand, letters used to denote furniture of Whitehall Palace.

Published by The Cobbe Collection Trust
in association with The National Trust ©2000
Printed in Great Britain by Surrey Litho Limited, Great Bookham, Surrey.
ISBN 0-9538203-0-0

CONTENTS

CATALOGUE

viii

Preface

Anyone who has a love of classical piano music will at some stage have wondered how the sound of our modern pianos compares with the sounds which the composers themselves enjoyed. The keyboard instruments now at Hatchlands have been gathered over a period of some thirty years with just such a question in mind. Amongst the myriads of sounds which have fallen into obscurity, the aim has been to seek those that appealed to and inspired the greatest composers. Most composers in history have been keyboard virtuosi. The keyboard instrument therefore has played roles as diverse as that of a private notebook, on which the most intimate musical thoughts were developed, to that of a formal platform on which the grandest compositions and virtuosic abilities of the masters of music have been displayed to the public.

It is therefore not surprising that the keyboard repertoire comprises one third of the whole of western music. Nor is it surprising that for many great composers, the relationship with their chosen keyboard-instrument maker was not merely professional but important in their personal lives as well.

This collection displays some thirty-seven instruments, all maintained in, or to be brought into, playing order - a fundamental object of The Cobbe Collection Trust, the charity which now owns and cares for the majority of them. They have been chosen to represent those instrument makers who were highly regarded or patronised by composers rather than to illustrate a complete or technical history of keyboard manufacture. Twelve of the instruments here were actually owned or almost certainly played by famous composers such as Purcell, J.C. Bach, Mozart, Beethoven, Chopin, Liszt, Mahler and Elgar - the largest group of such musical 'relics' to be seen in one place anywhere in the world.

It is obvious to any layman that in the case of a painting, the overall size, the colour and texture of paint employed by the artist are absolute and intrinsic qualities of the work of art. In musical connoisseurship, however, these seemingly simple fundamentals have been passed over. In the past, the education and training of pianists had tended little towards the history of their instrument. Thus for years the public have listened, unknowing and with equanimity, to keyboard works by composers of all periods performed on the same type of instrument; one furthermore whose tone in many cases bears little or no resemblance to any sound the composer himself ever heard. Even for the music from the height of the romantic era, the modern piano sound, with its long, clean and liquid notes, is far removed from the rich and romantic timbre of the instruments of the time. It is a fact that the masterpieces of instrument-building in early nineteenth century Vienna, the era of Beethoven and Schubert, had capabilities of shading, subtlety, and colour change that are considerably diminished in the modern factory-produced instrument.

The purpose of this catalogue is to show why each instrument was acquired and why it was exciting either in its history or its associations, as well as in its construction and design. Inevitably this approach is likely to produce something of a personal ideology.

It is the further aim of our Trustees to provide musicians and audiences with opportunities of experiencing the sounds of what music once was, in its many and magnificent varieties.

It is now over a decade since Martin Drury first put to me the suggestion that the collection be housed at Hatchlands, a property given to The National Trust in 1944 with few contents. The setting of the instruments in rooms designed by Robert Adam in the mid-eighteenth century, which I have hung with inherited and collected works of art, surrounded by parkland laid out by Humphrey Repton adds satisfyingly to the pleasure they give. Furthermore the rooms have a fine natural acoustic, none more so than the music room, designed in 1903 by Sir Reginald Blomfield, where our concerts take place. Its rounded ceiling and walls broken up by ornament are features that have, in recent times, come to be recognised as contributory to good acoustics. The number of visitors to the house, the collections and concerts has nearly quadrupled in these years which speaks well for the success of what is perhaps for the National Trust a somewhat unusual partnership.

Alec Cobbe
Hatchlands 1999

Hatchlands seen from across the park planted by Humphrey Repton.

David Mees

Acknowledgements

Most of the instruments were unplayable when acquired. That they now can be heard in all their wonderful variety is due to the skills, patience and scholarship of the restorers who have worked on them. In this connection it is appropriate to mention the long association, now of nearly twenty-five years duration, of David Hunt with the pianofortes of this collection. In the Fitzwilliam Catalogue of 1983 I paid tribute, as I do now, to his unfailing high standards and sensitivity. Others whose work on the collection has been especially valuable are David Baker, Peter Bavington, Edward Bennett, Ulrich Gerhartz, Martin Goetze, Claire Hammett, Miles Hellon, Darryl Martin, Chris Nobbs, Mark Ransom and David Winston.

In the preparation of this publication and in matters relating to the collection generally I have been helped in various ways by numerous people either personally or through their publications; Derek Adlam, Harry Ashbee, Alfred Brendel, Charles Cator, Michael Cole, Edward Corp, Hugh Dickinson, Martin Drury, Jutta Fischer, The Duke of Grafton, Edmond de la Haye Jousselin, Alison Hoskyns, Gilbert Kaplan, John Koster, Joan Lane, Michael Latcham, Richard Luckett, Richard Maunder, Donald Mitchell, Rose Monson, Charles Mould, Georgina Naylor, Chris Nobbs, David Owen-Norris, Grant O'Brien, Ian Pleeth, Stewart Pollens, Hugh Roberts, David Robinson, Albi Rosenthal, Christopher Rowell, David Rowlands, Alan Rubin, Hugh and Bridget Sackville West, Rosalind Savill, George Sayn, Andras Schiff, Mischa Scorer, Cindy and Houston Shaw Stewart, Mitsuko Uchida, Robert Venables, Jeremy Warren, Elizabeth Wells and Lance Whitehead, David Winston.

For the abundant illustrations in this book, I thank John Challis, Christopher Hurst, and David Mees.

In writing this work I am much indebted to the Chairman and Trustees of The Cobbe Collection Trust, to my brother, Hugh Cobbe, Music Librarian of the British Library, to Oliver Davies, Keeper of Portraits at The Royal College of Music, to Hugh Roberts, Director of the Royal Collection Trust and to my colleague David Mees for their kind help and ideas at all stages.

A Short Note on the Origins of Keyboard Instruments

There are various views concerning the evolution of keyboard instruments. Most authorities are agreed that the **organ,** said to have been invented in the third century B.C. by Ktesibios of Alexandria, predated the other forms of keyboard instrument by a very long way. Known as 'water-organs', they functioned by means of air driven through the pipes by hydraulic action. They may have derived from a device used in ancient Egypt to warn field workers of impending discharge from irrigation tanks. The instrument was adopted by the Emperors of the Eastern Roman Empire, but with pneumatic, rather than hydraulic, action using bellows. In this form it was re-introduced to the western world around the mid-sixth century A.D. One view is that this was achieved in the Christian west by Irish monks and scholars. There is evidence of an organ in the church at Clogher, Ireland, destroyed by fire in 814. References also exist to a famous instrument with four hundred pipes and seventy blowers, requiring two players, built for Winchester Cathedral sometime between 984 and 1005.

The earliest written references to **harpsichords**, known then as eschaquiers (literally chessboards, possibly on account of the chequered character of the keyboard itself) come at a rather later date. A reference to an *Eschaquier d'Engleterre* occurs in the writing of the Frenchman Machaut c. 1300-1377, whilst Edward III of England in 1360 gave an *echiquier* to his captive, King John of France. It is by no means certain however that the term *eschaquier* refers to a harpsichord or clavichord. Whether or not the harpsichord was an English invention, the world's earliest known manuscript of keyboard music is certainly an English document of c. 1325-50, bound in the Codex from Robertsbridge Abbey. The dance movements, termed 'estampies', are of French or Italian derivation. The world's earliest extant harpsichord is an upright instrument thought to have been made in Ulm c. 1480, and now in the museum of the Royal College of Music, London.

It is probably safe to assume that the **clavichord**, which has the simplest action of all keyboard instruments is at least as old as the harpsichord, and may predate it. Representations of both harpsichords and clavichords occur regularly in illuminated manuscripts, sculptures and stained glass from the first quarter of the fifteenth century onwards.

The **virginals** is a rectangular form of harpsichord, and probably of later development. On account of its modest size it was immensely popular as a domestic instrument in the sixteenth and seventeenth centuries both in Northern countries and in Italy. The title page of the first printed English keyboard music, *Parthenia*, published in 1612, depicts a lady playing a virginals. The name of the instrument may well derive from its association with female players.

Until recent years the **pianoforte** had been considered to have been invented by Bartolomeo Cristofori in Florence during the closing years of the seventeenth century. He termed his instrument *cembalo con piano e forte*. Reviews of early documents carried out by Stewart Pollens, however, indicate quite clearly that cembalos *con piano e forte* existed in Italy during the sixteenth century. Furthermore, drawings in a manuscript of Arnaut Zwolle, writing in Dijon c. 1440, illustrate different keyboard actions amongst which is one that Pollens has confidently interpreted as a striking action in a harpsichord-shaped instrument, this action being the defining characteristic of a pianoforte. The world's earliest extant pianoforte is an instrument by Cristofori dated 1720, now in the Metropolitan Museum, New York.

The Evolution of the Action of the Pianoforte

Unlike the harpsichord family of instruments whose action has remained largely unchanged for centuries, the piano action evolved dramatically during the two hundred and eighty years represented by surviving examples. This period saw the appearance of much of the classical repertoire for the instrument. This is a complex subject but the following attempts to give a simplified account of how two major types of action emerged during the eighteenth century and continued to dominate the tastes of composers and pianists for much of the nineteenth.

The earliest pianofortes to survive are the 'revival' instruments from the 1720's of Cristofori who developed a very sophisticated action. This has the hammers mounted on a rail above the keylevers and pointing *away* from the player. Cristofori's 1726 action was used virtually unmodified by the Saxon maker Gottfried Silbermann in his surviving instruments of the 1740's. It would seem that he had observed an actual instrument, brought perhaps by one of the Italian musicians at the Dresden Court, as the particular action he copied was not, so far as we know, published during his lifetime. Silbermann's nephew, Johann Heinrich Silbermann of Strasburg, used a modified version of Cristofori's action in a surviving instrument of 1776.

Another action in use in Germany in primitive form and which may have evolved from modification of clavichords into pianofortes, was termed *prellmechanik*. Here the hammer was pivoted within a wooden housing termed a *kapsel* mounted on the keylever itself, and pointed *towards* the player. It was a pupil of J.H. Silbermann, Johann Andreas Stein, who probably invented and certainly perfected this action. He was the maker of the earliest surviving grand pianoforte, c.1775, incorporating it. Stein's huge success with these instruments ensured that this action was universally adopted throughout the Germanies and Austria extinguishing entirely the type of piano developed by Silbermann. This action was used by all the classic Viennese makers and came to be termed **Viennese Action**.

When piano-building commenced during the 1760's in England, however, it was the Cristofori type of action with the hammer pointing *away* from the player which was again the model. Although many German makers arrived in the British Isles none, excepting perhaps Ferdinand Weber, seem to have had any demonstrable links with Silbermann's work. Zumpe, the most successful of them, scored his triumphs with a square piano action that was a very simplified form of the Cristofori system. The one surviving model of grand pianoforte developed by Americus Backers perhaps as early as the 1760's, has an action modified from Cristofori, though, it would seem, without knowledge of what the Silbermanns had achieved. Michael Cole has identified evidence of the presence of Florentine pianofortes in London on which Backers and Zumpe could have based their work. Zumpe's square piano action, though it was later radically improved, became the basis of those in square pianos for as long as they continued to be made. Backers' grand piano action was also the springboard for future developments. It was adopted by all English makers and became known as the **English Action**. In the 1790's it was taken up by Erard who for much of his life worked at improving it. He succeeded in developing a revolutionary action on which that of modern instruments is based. The Viennese action was all but extinct by the end of the nineteenth century.

Glossary of Terms

Buff stop: A stop where muting leathers, in series or in a single strip, butt against the strings to produce a 'pizzicato' effect when notes are played.

Clavichord: A stringed keyboard instrument at least as old as the harpsichord and perhaps earlier. It is usually constructed as a rectangular box, with the keyboard set into or projecting from one of the longer sides. It has the simplest possible action of any keyboard instrument: when a key is pressed, the far end raises a metal strip (known as a 'tangent') to touch the string. This makes the sound which continues while the contact is maintained. An increase in the pressure on the key while the note sounds will change the pitch of the note by stretching the string. The result is an instrument of great sensitivity which allows the player to obtain something of the 'vibrato' available to a violinist or guitarist. It is, however, a very quiet instrument.

Compass: The number of notes in an instrument. It is expressed either as a simple number, i.e. a compass of 58 notes, or more usually in octaves. Over the centuries the compass of instruments gradually increased and there were regional differences.

Escapement: An adjustable mechanism by which the hammer of a pianoforte is allowed to fall back immediately after impact with the string, even while the key is still depressed.

Double escapement: A sprung lever which supports the weight of the hammer momentarily after it has struck the string, allowing the escapement to reset *before* the key returns to rest, thus speeding up repetition significantly.

Fortepiano: A term sometimes used today for pianofortes made in the eighteenth and early nineteenth centuries, to distinguish them from later instruments. It was originally used arbitrarily by different makers alongside 'pianoforte'.

Grand Pianoforte (Grand Piano): A piano in a wing-shaped case of a form derived from the harpsichord. The earliest use of the term was in 1777, by Robert Stodart in describing a harpsichord-piano.

Harpsichord: A wing-shaped keyboard instrument. One of whose longer sides is usually curved. It may have one keyboard (called a 'single manual'), two (a 'double manual') or sometimes even three (a 'triple manual') and usually has up to 3 sets of strings per note. When a key is depressed, the far end of the key lever projects upwards a vertical wooden jack in which is mounted a small piece of quill, the **plectrum**, which plucks the string. The force by which the key is depressed has negligible effect on the resultant volume. The volume of sound can be increased by bringing into play, by mechanical means, additional sets of strings and jacks so that two or more strings are plucked when a key is depressed.

Jack: A small wooden device used in harpsichords, spinets and virginals to carry the quill or plectrum which plucks the strings. The quill is set in a pivoted tongue so that it does not pluck the string on its return journey. They are mounted vertically and are pushed upwards when the key is pressed. A **jack-rail** mounted above prevents them from flying out, and they rebound to their place.

Kapsel: A wooden or metal pronged device mounted on the keylever and between the prongs of which the hammer is pivoted.

Keywell: The space above the keyboards, the back of which is usually the nameboard, and the ends of which are frequently enclosed by treble and bass 'cheeks'.

Knee-lever: A lever placed under the main case of some keyboard instruments, which carries out the functions later given to pedals. These normally included a sustaining function still present on modern instruments and others could produce different effects when operated by the player's knee (thus keeping the hands free).

Pianoforte (Piano): Literally 'soft-loud', this is a keyboard instrument in which strings are struck by rebounding hammers rather than plucked (as in a harpsichord) or by 'tangents' (as in a clavichord). It has gained importance over other kinds of instruments for two main reasons. Firstly it can play both loud and soft, and can do so for different notes at the same time. Secondly it can play more notes than any other instrument and thus give an adapted rendering of any Western music.

Prellmechanik: A form of piano action where the hammer is mounted on the keylever.

Ravalement: A process of enlarging an instrument to give it a larger compass or number of notes than that with which it was originally built.

Spinet: A diminutive harpsichord which can be triangular or pentagonal in shape. The strings are usually at an angle to the keyboard.

Stop: A knob or lever on an instrument that is operated by hand and mechanically changes some aspect of the performance or sound quality of the instrument.

Tangent: See clavichord.

Virginals: A rectangular keyboard instrument with plucking action as in a harpsichord. Much in vogue in the sixteenth and the seventeenth centuries.

Wrestpin: Iron pins, one for each string, set in a robust plank, the wrestplank, round which the string is fixed by winding several times. The tension and thus the pitch of the string can be adjusted by slightly turning the wrestpin by means of a tuning key. In harpsichords and grand pianofortes the wrestplank is set at the front of the instrument just behind the nameboard.

The Catalogue

Technical data are given at the end of the entry for each instrument.
All dimensions are in millimetres. '3-Octave span' is the width of 21 naturals. Case sizes are of the main body of the instrument, excluding lid and mouldings. Since the treble cheeks of harpsichords and grand pianofortes are rarely parallel to the spine, the width is measured over the gap. Depth is measured at the centre of the treble cheek.

Unless otherwise stated, instruments were given by Alec Cobbe to The Cobbe Collection Trust in 1997.

1. HARPSICHORD

attributed to Girolamo Zenti, Viterbo, c.1622.

Zenti made several harpsichords for the Medici family during the 1630s in Florence, and the inventories of this great family in 1690 list six instruments by him. He also worked for Queen Christina of Sweden in Rome and Louis XIV at Versailles. In the year before his death he came briefly to London to work for Charles II. He returned to France shortly before he died in 1668. He is credited with the invention of the triangular spinet. Of the seven surviving instruments attributed to Zenti, this harpsichord is the earliest. It is of typical early Italian construction where a plain lightly-built instrument is enclosed in a quite separate, more robust and frequently decorative outer case. Instruments such as this occurred in the collection of the Italophile Henry VIII and would have been familiar to the English virginalists. The instrument, its outer case and stand are all original but they have clearly sustained changes in decoration; the painting inside the lid probably dates from c. 1680, and the external and soundboard decorations from c. 1740. The tone is lute-like and, for the size of the instrument, surprisingly resonant.

Provenance
College of Instrument Technology.
Acquired by Michael Thomas.
1989 Purchased by Alec Cobbe.
1997 Given to the Cobbe Collection Trust.

TECHNICAL DATA

Maker	Attributed to Girolamo Zenti of Viterbo.
Date	c. 1622

Inscriptions on lowest key and jack
    G.Z. 1622?: iGZ2?

Compass	C/E (short octave)-c^3. Single manual. Fruitwood naturals. Ebony-capped sharps.
3-Octave span	488
Registration	2x8'. 2 rows of jacks.

	C	c^2	c^3
Scaling	1575/1567	288/275	140/133
			Long8'/Short 8'
Pluck point	138/122	91/71	65/46
Gauges	0.30	0.23	0.2

Inner case	Cypress. Length 1923. Width 704. Depth 167.
Outer case	Length 1990. Width 746. Depth 197.
Restorations	Restrung by Darryl Martin in 1993

David Mees

1.1   Harpsicord, attributed to Girolamo Zenti, 1622.

2. HARPSICHORD
probably English, dated 1623.

The gift of the Iliffe Family.

This very richly decorated instrument came from Coker Court, Somerset, where it had long been in the ownership of the Helyar family and later, through the marriage of the last of the Helyars, the Heneage families. Present members of the family confirm it to have been a Helyar rather than a Heneage chattel. Dr William Helyar, Archdeacon of Exeter purchased Coker Court in 1616 and died in 1645. Helyar's heir was his grandson, another William, who lost his lands in the civil war but regained them in 1648 on payment of a fine, and survived in prosperity until 1697. Thus either William might have been the first owner of the present instrument.

2.2 Detail of soundboard showing original gilt border decoration and date of 1623.

Michael Thomas, who purchased the instrument from the family in the 1950s remembered reports of it being mentioned in eighteenth century inventories of the house, though recent perusal of Coker Court records has not confirmed this. While it is probably of English manufacture, the possibility of a Flemish origin could be considered. The date of the instrument has been much questioned.

The gilt and gesso numerals '1623' on the soundboard are certainly part of the original decorative scheme. However makers in the seventeenth and eighteenth centuries were not above passing off their work as being older than it actually was. The size and compass of the instrument (originally 58 notes) and the character of the floral soundboard decoration have led some historians to the conclusion that the instrument dates from the eighteenth century, though there is a late seventeenth century example of a Couchet harpsichord with a compass of 59 notes. Technical examination of the soundboard shows the floral decoration to be a second generation scheme probably dating from around 1720-30. This was achieved by eradicating the original decoration but leaving intact the original borders and date. The 'new' floral decoration has been considered by Grant O'Brien to bear a resemblance to the work of the painter of the 'Ham House Ruckers' -

2.1 Painted panel on the side of the instrument.

David Mees

2.3   The richly decorated harpsicord, probably English, inscribed with the date of 1623.

an English forgery of the 1730s.

The exterior of the instrument is decorated with tulips, particularly fashionable in the decorative arts around the middle of the seventeenth century. Furthermore, analysis of original pigments on the exterior of the case strongly suggests seventeenth century origins, in which case the instrument may be the earliest surviving playable English harpsichord.

Provenance
Helyar family at Coker Court, Somerset.
1950s Purchased from Mrs. Heneage by Michael Thomas.
c.1989 Sold to Dr. Andreas Beurmans.
1995 Purchased by the Iliffe Family Trust.
1997 Given to The Cobbe Collection Trust.

TECHNICAL DATA

Date	c.1623
Soundboard Inscription	
	1623
Compass	5 Octaves, F_1/G_1- f^3. Double manual. Originally Ivory naturals and ebony capped sharps.
3-Octave-span	469.

2.4   The Great Hall at Coker Court, Somerset (c.1950), showing the 1623 harpsicord on the right. Courtesy of Simon Heneage.

Registration	2x8',1x4' and Lute. 4 Rows of jacks.		
Scaling 1997	F_1	c^2	f^3
8'	1607/1599	349/330	115/104
			Long8'/Short8'
Pluck-point	236/197	112/72	84/51
Gauges	0.56	0.25	0.19

Stops	4 Handstops: Back 8', 4', Lute, Front 8'
Case	Painted pine. Length 2150. Width 908. Depth 259
Restorations	No major restoration work since acquisition.

3. HARPSICHORD
by Andreas Ruckers, Antwerp, 1636.
Ravalement by Henri Hemsch, Paris, 1763.

The Ruckers family of Antwerp (Hans, his two sons Ioannes and Andreas, his two grandsons, Andreas Ruckers II and Ioannes Couchet) can be considered to be the greatest of all harpsichord makers. Their instruments achieved a richness of sound that was never equalled, before or since, and held a position of unrivalled supremacy from their own time until the end of the eighteenth century when harpsichord-building came to an end. So fine was the reputation of their instruments that they received orders from several European monarchs, including Charles I whose instrument was sent to be decorated by Rubens, a few streets away from their workshops.

By the middle of the eighteenth century Ruckers harpsichords were more sought after than contemporary ones, in preference even to those by the best makers. Accordingly (as with this instrument) they were enlarged to provide the extra notes required by the contemporary repertoire, a process known as *ravalement*. In mid-eighteenth century Paris, when the price of a new harpsichord stood at around five hundred livres, an Andreas Ruckers harpsichord was offered for twenty thousand. Such high values led some otherwise perfectly respectable instrument-makers to

John Challis

3.1 Ruckers-Hemsch, 1636.

John Challis

3.2   Ruckers-Hemsch,1636, rose and soundboard decoration.

produce dubious transformations of Ruckers fragments into full size pieces or even to make outright forgeries of Ruckers instruments. An example of the latter can be seen at Ham House (a property of The National Trust) where a harpsichord, by an unknown early eighteenth century English maker of high quality, is deliberately decorated to resemble a Ruckers instrument, complete with maker's 'inscription'.

The Ruckers were highly esteemed in eighteenth-century England. Their construction profoundly influenced the output of Jacob Kirkman and Burkat Shudi, London's two leading harpsichord-makers of the time, who were both trained by the same master, a pupil of the Couchet workshop. Handel's preferred instrument was his Ruckers harpsichord which he kept at his house in Brook Street. Burkat Shudi also kept two Ruckers harpsichords which were regularly hired out by the firm until as late as the 1790s.

As well as inspiring composers, makers and monarchs, in more recent times Ruckers instruments have also fired the energies of instrument historians. Alfred Hipkins, perhaps the most distinguished early historian of keyboard instruments, provided the Ruckers entry for the first edition of Grove's *Dictionary of Music and Musicians* in 1883. In it he wrote:

It is certain that the tone of Ruckers harpsichords has never been surpassed for purity and beauty of tone-colour…..Time seemed to have no effect with the ….instruments. They were decorated with costly paintings in this country and in France, when a hundred years old and more. New keys and new jacks replaced the old ones; so long as the soundboard stood lasted the 'silvery sweet' tone…..but modern conditions of life seem to be inimical to the old wood; it will be difficult, if not impossible, to preserve any of the old instruments much

3.4   Ruckers-Hemsch,1636, lowest keylever, showing inscribed date of *Ravalement*, 1763.

longer. As a work of piety we have catalogued all that we have seen or can hear of, appending the list to this notice.

Hipkins listed, with short descriptions, all surviving Ruckers instruments that he could discover, the first study of its kind in the history of western musical instruments. It prompted later ambitious works embracing all surviving historical harpsichords by named makers by Donald Boalch, and pianofortes up to 1820 by Martha Clinkscale, both published by the

3.3   Ruckers-Hemsch,1636, keyboards and keywell.

3.5   Ruckers-Hemsch, 1636.

Oxford University Press. Hipkins' initiative on the Ruckers *œuvre* was to be followed over a century later by a matchless monograph on this remarkable family of makers by Grant O'Brien, incorporating a very full and definitive catalogue of their surviving instruments.

This instrument was built in 1636 with a single manual and the Flemish landscape painting on the inside of the lid dates from this period. By the end of the seventeenth century the instrument seems to have reached France where the soundboard decoration was beautifully re-done in a finer manner than was normal in the Ruckers' own workshop practice. A major enlargement was carried out by Henri Hemsch in 1763 when a second manual was added, a new stand provided and the external decorations completely and attractively renewed. This work is accepted as Hemsch's by both the character of the keyboards and the additional painted decoration on the keywell, jackrail and soundboard, which has been identified as being by 'The Hemsch painter'. The original landscape on the inside of lid was retained by Hemsch, the extension in length being neatly achieved by the insertion of a strip of wood painted with an extra tree. A coat of arms, probably that of the patron for whom the *ravalement* was carried out, is incorporated in the external decoration but it has so far defied identification. Hemsch was one of the leading Paris makers. He supplied and tuned instruments for Rameau's patron *fermier général* M. Le Riche de La Pouplinière in whose house Rameau lived for a decade. This is a harpsichord well-known for its extraordinarily beautiful sound, handsomely fulfilling the legendary reputation of Ruckers' instruments.

Provenance

The instrument is believed to have belonged to the Savoy family.

In 1883 what appears to have been this instrument was recorded in Dijon, France by E. van der Straeten for Hipkins. In Hipkins' list it is numbered 71 and the description given is as follows: Form: bent side, Date: 1636, 2 keyboards not original; 5 octaves; black naturals stops and legs like Taskin's; beautifully painted. Inscribed ANDREAS RUCKERS ME FECIT ANTVERPIÆ with date.

By 1971 noted by the Comtesse de Chambure as being in the possession of Dr. Stefanovitch, Menton. France.

Sometime after 1971 the Comtesse de Chambure acquired the instrument on behalf of the French national collections to be swapped with Michael Thomas in return for his harpsichord of 1779 by Sébastian Erard. The latter instrument was purchased by Thomas from the Astor family at Hever following the flood of 1968 in which it had disassembled whilst under water. (For another instrument which survived this flood see No. 12).

1989-1992 acquired from Michael Thomas by Alec Cobbe.

1997 Given to The Cobbe Collection Trust.

TECHNICAL DATA

Date	1636
Nameboard Inscription	
	ANDREAS RVCKERS ME FECIT ANTVERPIÆ 1636
Inscription on F_1 *lower keyboard*	1763
Compass	5 Octaves, F_1-f^3. Double manual. Ebony naturals. Bone-capped sharps. Originally single manual C-c^3.
3-Octave span	477
Registration	2x8',1x4'. 3 rows of jacks.

	F_1	c^2	f^3
8' Scaling	1621/1613	362/346	141/133 Long8'/Short8'
Pluck point	229/183	115/75	86/41
Gauges	0.56	0.23	0.15
4' Scaling	980	172	72
Pluck point	119	42	34

Stops	Keyboard coupler by sliding upper keyboard. 3 Hand-stops: Buff (on slide), Back 8' (left), 4'(right)
Case	Painted poplar. Length 2140. Width 895. Depth 278.
Restorations	No major work since acquisition.

4. VIRGINALS

by John Player, London, 1664.

Probably from the Court of King Charles II at Whitehall Palace.

This instrument may be a unique musical survival from the Royal Household of Charles II. The letters 'WP' branded on its left front panel were those used to mark Whitehall Palace chattels and its builder's practice had supplied instruments to the Royal Household through two generations.

John Player was born in Gloucestershire around 1634. His business originated in that of John Hasard, who in 1612 is listed as receiving a royal stipend as instrument-tuner to Princess Elizabeth, sister of Charles I. In that year William Byrd and others dedicated the first English printed keyboard music, *Parthenia*, to the same Princess. Hasard's only known surviving work is the famous harpsichord of 1622, of which only the lidless case survives now at Knole. After his death the patronage of Princess Elizabeth (later known as the Winter Queen) was extended to his son-in-law Gabriel Townsend, whose only surviving instrument is a virginals made for his royal Patroness. John Player was Townsend's senior apprentice at the time of his death and had 'inherited' his business by 1660. This, his only surviving virginals, bears a brand WP, letters used to mark furniture for Whitehall Palace. This was the year of the Restoration, and one of the earliest of the new King's projects was to re-establish the Royal Musick. He had always remained close to his musical Aunt who had accompanied him back to England, and nothing would have been more likely than her directing him to the instrument makers she had patronised all her life.

In 1673 the instruments at Whitehall, and in the Royal Household, came under the care of the young Henry Purcell who was appointed 'keeper, mender, maker, repairer, and tuner of the regals, organs, virginals… to His Majesty'. The routine maintenance of this instrument may well, therefore, have been carried out by the composer.

4.1   Virginals by John Player, 1664.

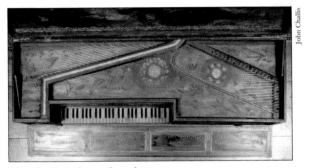

4.2   The Virginals seen from above.

4.3   Detail showing the WP brand.

Although a Virginals possesses the same plucking mechanism as a harpsichord, it is of rectangular shape. The jacks and plectra must therefore emerge through apertures in the soundboard to pluck the strings. In a harpsichord the jacks are situated outside the soundboard area altogether. Around twenty-four English virginals survive today and in general they have larger compasses than their European counterparts. They represent a flourishing tradition of instrument-building from a period when English composers were leaders in the development of keyboard technique and composition.

The recently discovered manuscript of keyboard music by Purcell, now in the British Library, was recorded by Virgin Classics entirely on this instrument, performed by Davitt Moroney. It is available at Hatchlands.

4.4 Detail showing name batten.

4.5 Detail of keywell and keyboard.

4.6 Detail of one of the roses.

Provenance
Captain Lane of Wanstead.
Sold at Sotheby's November 1955.
Bought by Raymond Russell.
1957 Acquired by the Gemeentemuseum, The Hague.
1991 De-accessioned and sold to Alec Cobbe.
1992 Exhibited February-April in the King's Library at the British Museum.
1997 Given to the Cobbe Collection Trust.

Restored to playing order with the assistance of a grant from Booz. Allen & Hamilton.

TECHNICAL DATA

Date	1664
Nameboard Inscription	
	Iohannis Player Londini Me Fecit 1664
Case Inscription	W P.
Compass	4½ Octaves, Chromatic as indicated G_1-d^3.
	Fruitwood naturals. Stained sharps.
3-Octave span	486
Registration	1x8'.

	G_1	c^2	d^3
Scaling	1578	301	130
Pluck point	142	61	41
Gauges	0.35	0.25	0.23

Case	Painted pine and oak.
	Length 1786. Width 526. Depth 215.
	The top and front lids and the sides are nineteenth century replacements.
	The stand is of recent date.
Restorations	Restored to working order by Darryl Martin and Chris Nobbs in 1992

5. CHAMBER ORGAN
by John Snetzler, London, 1759.

Johann Snetzler was Swiss-born and had emigrated to London by 1740. He rapidly became one of the leading organ-builders in the capital. In 1760 he is said to have made an organ for George III, believed to be that which survives today in Eton College Chapel. Snetzler tended to standardise the outward appearance of his chamber instruments, but the outer cases of the Eton and Hatchlands organs are both made to exceptional designs.

Sherbourne Park, for which it is believed this organ was made, had been inhabited by the Webb family prior to the death of Elias Webb in 1727. His grandson, John, set about rebuilding it between 1754 and 1758, when the new house was ready for furnishing. Whilst lesser furniture was made by local craftsmen the important pieces were ordered from London during 1758 and 1759. No records relating to this organ have been identified amongst the quite detailed Webb papers surviving in the Nottingham Record Office; but it does seem very likely that the organ was amongst the items ordered then. It was certainly in the possession of the Smith Ryland family after their purchase of Sherbourne in 1830.

Chamber organs such as this played an important role in Handel's musical life. He used them, during the intervals of his operas, to perform the world's first orchestral organ concertos, and in 1742 he went to the trouble of taking a chamber organ, said to have been made by Snetzler, on his journey to Dublin, for use in the first performance of the Messiah.

Provenance
1759 Made for John Webb at Sherbourne Park, Warwickshire (?).
1916 Transferred by the Smith-Rylands to Wellesbourne Methodist Chapel.
1988 Sold from the chapel by tender, through Ian Pleeth, to Alec Cobbe.
1997 Given to The Cobbe Collection Trust.

C. Barda, London

5.1   Organ by John Schnetzler, 1759.

Martin Goetze

5.2   Detail of label within the instrument showing Schnetzler's signature.

TECHNICAL DATA

Date	1759
Pallet Box	—— Snetzler fecit Londini
Inscription	1759
Compass	5 Octaves, G_1/A_1 - f^3. Single manual. Divided at b/c^1. Ebony naturals. Ivory-capped sharps.
3-Octave-span	484.
Action	Mechanical with backfalls.
Registration	9 Stops:

Stop Diapason	Wood	
Open Diapason	c^1-f^3	
Dulciana	c-f^3	
Principal Bass		
Principal Treble		
Flute	Wood	
Fifteenth		
Sesquialtera Bass	1996	
Cornet Treble	1996	

2 Pedals:
  Shifting movement leaves only
  Diapasons, Dulciana and Flute.
  Venetian swell.

Wind supply	Hand or foot pump, plus Electric blower 55mm (1996).
Outer Case	Mahogany. Height c.3100. Width c.1700. Depth c.1000.
Restorations	Restored to working order by M Goetze and D Gwynn in 1996.

6. SQUARE PIANOFORTE
by Johannes Zumpe and Gabriel Buntebart, London, 1769.

Johannes Zumpe was born in 1726 at Fürth near Nuremberg. He was apprenticed as a cabinet-maker, but left his home town shortly after 1750. On arrival in London he came to work in the establishment of the harpsichord-maker, Burkat Shudi. By 1761 he had set up his own workshop in Princes Street where he seems to have been principally a maker of guitars and where he was visited by the Mozart family in 1764.

Zumpe's important place in history, however, derives from his apparent invention of the square piano, sometime before 1766. At this time piano manufacture in London was otherwise confined to the experimental work being carried out on grand pianofortes, i.e. those of harpsichord shape, chiefly by Americus Backers. These two men virtually laid the foundations of the English school of pianoforte-building.

It was the relatively inexpensive square piano, however, that captivated the imagination of the English music-loving public, and Zumpe's instruments became widely sought-after and were exported all over Europe. He is the first piano-maker in history to achieve international success.

A square piano from Zumpe is likely to have cost in the region of £20 as opposed to the £80 cost of a harpsichord from Kirkman or Shudi. However, the ultimate triumph of Zumpe's invention was due in no small part to the arrival of Johann Sebastian Bach's youngest son, Johann Christian, in London in 1762. This favourite son had grown up at a time when his father was developing a considerable interest in the pianos of Gottfried Silbermann. He was now to become a champion of Zumpe's square pianos.

Johann Christian Bach's 'Solo on the Piano Forte' advertised at the Thatched House, St. James's in June 1768 is the first documented public performance of the

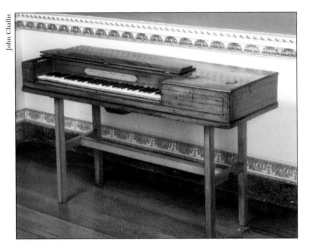

6.1   Square Pianoforte by Johannes Zumpe and Gabriel Buntebart, 1769.

6.2   The instrument seen from above.

6.3   Detail of the nameboard.

piano used as a solo instrument in England. The composers's bank account for July 1768 records a payment of £50 to Zumpe, probably representing purchases of instruments, one of which may have been used in that performance. At that time, Johann Christian Bach's fame and success exceeded that achieved by any other member of his family, his music being performed all over Europe.

It seems extraordinary to us today that these tiny but sweet sounding instruments were to pose such a profound musical challenge to the powerful harpsichords at the time, but the value placed by musicians on the possibilities of note by note inflection given by Zumpe's instruments must have been very great.

Provenance
Purchased by Ian Pleeth.
1979 Purchased from him by Alec Cobbe.
1983 Exhibited The Fitzwilliam Museum, Cambridge, *A Century of Keyboard Instruments*, No. 4.
1991 Exhibited The British Library, London
Mozart: 'Prodigy of Nature'.
1997 Given to The Cobbe Collection Trust.

TECHNICAL DATA

Date	1769
Nameboard	Johannes Zumpe) Londini Fecit [sic] 1769
Inscription	et Buntebart.) *Princes Street Hanover*
	Square
Compass	5 Octaves (short), G_1-f^3 (Dummy G_1#).
	Ivory naturals. Ebony-capped sharps.
3-Octave span	485
Stringing	Bichord throughout.

	G_1	c^2	f^3
Scaling	1047	293	99
Strike point	55	23	10
Gauges	Spun	0.36	0.36

Action	English single. Overdampers throughout.
Stops	3 Hand-stops:
	Two for divided dampers.
	Buff.
Case	Solid Mahogany.
	Length 1265. Width 470. Depth 159.
Restorations	Restored to working order in 1982.

7. HARPSICHORD

by Jacob and Abraham Kirkman, London, 1772.

The property of Mr. Alec Cobbe.

Harpsichord-building in London during the eighteenth century was dominated by two great makers, Jacob Kirkman from Alsace and the Swiss-born Burkhardt Tschudi, who anglicised his name to Burkat Shudi. Both learned from the same master, Hermann Tabel, who had been apprenticed to the Ruckers/Couchet workshops in Antwerp. Following Tabel's death, Kirkman gained something of an advantage over his rival by marrying Tabel's widow

David Mees

7.1   Double manual harpsichord by Jacob and Abraham Kirkman.

and thereby acquiring all the seasoned timber and customers of a very successful business.

Not unnaturally the two makers built their instruments on somewhat similar lines, and both responded to the increasing popularity of the pianoforte by bringing devices to the harpsichord to achieve crescendo and diminuendo effects. The harpsichord here is fitted with a pedal which, when depressed, raises a flap of the lid to obtain a greater volume of sound. This mechanism was known as a 'Nag's head swell' because of the resemblance that the profile of the opened lid flap bears to a horse's head and neck.

Kirkman's instruments were very highly thought of. Indeed, George III traded a Ruckers harpsichord to acquire one of Kirkman's double manual instruments for Queen Charlotte. His business acumen is vividly illustrated by his reaction to an increasing infatuation of fashionable ladies to the 'English Guittar'. He bought up a large quantity of the guitars and distributed them freely to milliners and ladies of the street. The craze was quickly abandoned by society.

The cost of a very fine Kirkman instrument is recorded in the maker's bill to the family at Nostell Priory where the instrument supplied survives:

Sir Rowland Winn Bart. Dr to Jacob Kirkman September ye 1st 1767. An Inlaid Double Keyed Harpsichord Cover veneered Desk inside with machine pedals 85 guineas £ 89.5. Leather Cover for Do £ 1. 10. Packing Case for Do £ - . 15 . Total £ 91. 10.

From Kirkman's marriage, to a lady one presumes to have been very much older than himself, there were no children. He was joined and succeeded in his firm by his nephew Abraham, who took this very distinguished name well into the age of pianofortes.

Provenance
Purchased by Ian Pleeth at Sotheby's London 26th November 1992.
1997 Purchased from Ian Pleeth by Alec Cobbe.

TECHNICAL DATA

Date	1772
Nameboard Inscription	
	Jacobus et Abraham Kirkman Londini fecerunt 1772.
Compass	5 Octaves, F_1/G_1 - f^3. Double manual. Replacement Ivory naturals and Ebony sharps.
3-Octave-span	Keylevers replacements.
Registration	2x8',1x4' and Lute. 4 Rows of jacks.

	F_1	c^2	f^3
8' Scaling	1743/1735	347/335	133/128 Long8'/Short8'
Pluck-point	185/201	81/96	50/66
Lute			
Pluck-point	74	24	15
Gauges	0.6	0.23	0.23
Gauges Marked	13	4	4

Stops	5 Handstops plus Machine handstop:	
	(left)	(right)
	Buff	Front 8'
	Lute	Back 8'
	4'	
	2 Pedals: Machine	'Nag's head' swell
Case	Mahogany veneered oak.	
	Length 2340. Width 938. Depth 317.	
Restorations	The keys, jacks and stand were made in the restoration of 1996	

8. SQUARE PIANOFORTE
by Johannes Zumpe and Gabriel Buntebart, London, 1777-78. The soundboard autographed by Johann Christian Bach.

This instrument survived in a family house in a village near Saint Germain-en-Laye. It was almost certainly brought to France by Johann Christian Bach when he visited that town, accompanied by Mozart, in August 1778. He had arrived there to stay with the Duc de Noailles, the Maréchal of Saint Germain, who was one of the most important musical patrons in the country. We know of Bach's visit to Saint Germain only from a letter that Mozart wrote to his father. On his way through Paris, Bach had encountered the younger composer, then in mourning for his mother, and generously suggested that he should accompany with him.

At this date French piano-building was in its infancy, the fortepianos in Paris being mostly imported from London, and it is likely that Bach thought it necessary to bring a London instrument with him. He might have been asked to do so by the Duc de Noailles for in at least two instances Bach is known to have received requests from a friend, Denis Diderot, and a pupil, Madame Brillon, in Paris to choose a London piano for them. In each case he selected a Zumpe piano.

It is most probable that this piano was present whilst the two composers were guests of the Duc de Noailles. It would have been used for much of the music making described by Mozart and may well have rendered the first performance by the latter of his great sonata K.310 in A minor.

The Maréchal was clearly on good terms with the town, for when the revolution came, instead of his house being sacked it was merely confiscated and immediately leased back to him on terms from which his sons could benefit after him. It was not until the 1840's when a new road was planned to run through the centre of the building that the contents of the house were dispersed and the building partially demolished. Miraculously the Duc de Noailles' beautiful Salon de Musique, in which this historic week of music took place, survives in the fragments of the Hôtel de Noailles, still standing on either side of a street in Saint Germain.

The instrument shows considerable advances in size and quality of sound on the earlier instrument by Zumpe described above (No. 6).

Provenance
1778 probably brought to France by Johann Christian Bach and taken on his visit to St. Germain-en-Laye in the company of Mozart.
Possibly Hôtel de Noailles, St. Germain-en-Laye(?) until sale of contents c.1840.
Family at Marne la Coquette, near St. Germaine-en-Laye, since living memory.
Sold at auction (signature unobserved), bought by Robert Cardo who identified the inscription.
1994 Purchased from him by Alec Cobbe.
1997 Given to The Cobbe Collection Trust.

TECHNICAL DATA

Date	c. 1778
Nameboard Inscription	
	Original nameboard missing.
Soundboard Inscription	
	J C Bach
Compass	5 Octaves, F_1/G_1 - f^3.
	Ivory naturals. Ebony capped sharps.
3-Octave-span	484.
Hammers	Original coverings on all original hammers (15 hammers replaced)
Stringing	Bichord throughout.

	F_1	c^2	f^3
Scaling	1288	315	104
Strike-point	84	27	19
Gauges	Spun	.36	.36

Action	English single. Overdampers throughout.
Stops	3 Hand-stops:
	Two for divided dampers.
	Buff.
Case	Solid Mahogany.
	Length 1459. Width 515. Depth 184.
Restorations	Restored to working order in 1994.

Restored to playing order with the assistance of a grant from Sarasin Investment Management Ltd.

Chris Hurst

8.1   Square pianoforte by Johannes Zumpe and Gabriel Buntebart, 1777-78.

David Hunt

8.2   Detail of Johann Christian Bach's signature on the soundboard.

9. SPINET

by Ferdinand Weber, Dublin, 1780.

Signed on underside of the soundboard

'Ferdinand Weber fecit Dublin 1780'.

The property of Trustees for the Cobbe family collection.

Ferdinand Weber was born near Meissen, and was apprenticed there from 1728-1735 to Johann Hahnel, a clavichord-maker and organ-builder to the Court of Saxony at Dresden. This was a very interesting time and place for a young aspiring keyboard-maker. The piano-making activities of Gottfried Silbermann, who was also organ-builder to the Court and whose workshop was close by at Freiburg im Meissen, had come to maturity in 1732. In this year he presented one of his new *piano-fort* instruments to The Elector of Saxony at the Dresden Court and, it is also thought, sent one to his friend Johann Sebastian Bach in Leipzig. Bach certainly seems to have been in possession of Silbermann *piano-forts* from 1733, a circumstance that was, perhaps, a significant factor in the enthusiasm for the instrument of his youngest son, Johann Christian.

It is inconceivable that a fellow builder at Court and his apprentices would not have been closely abreast of these developments, and it can be no coincidence that Weber was the probable introducer of the pianoforte into Ireland. Hahnel is certainly documented as having involved himself in the manufacture and development of the *Cembalo d'Amour*, a kind of clavichord of Silbermann's invention.

With this illustrious beginning Weber emigrated to England where he spent about a year and was in Dublin by 1749. He quickly became the most sought-after builder of organs and harpsichords in the capital. He made a harpsichord for Thomas Roseingrave, friend of

9.1   Spinet by Ferdinand Weber, 1778.

Domenico Scarlatti and introducer of the latter's music to the British Isles. One of Weber's own account ledgers survives in manuscript copy, giving detailed information concerning the supply and tuning of harpsichords, 'Spinnets' and 'Forte Pianos' going back to 1764. This may well be one of the earliest detailed keyboard instrument-maker's accounts of this kind to survive in Europe. The ledger also shows that Weber ran a thriving trade importing porcelain.

Weber's name appears in the account books of the Cobbe family at Newbridge House, near Dublin, which record that he became the supplier and tuner of instruments there in 1756. The maker's own ledger shows Lady Betty Cobbe to have been a considerable client, possessing a 'Spinnet', two harpsichords, and from 1775 a 'Forte Piano'. Her patronage was of nearly thirty years duration.

Ireland had not been slow in adopting the 'new instrument', for the first recorded public solo

9.2   Weber's signature and date on underside of soundboard.

9.3   Detail of nameboard.

performance on a pianoforte in Dublin, on the 19th May 1768, predates that of Johann Christian Bach in London by a month. It was given by Henry Walsh, organist of St. Patrick's Cathedral and Lady Betty Cobbe's harpsichord teacher. The common patronage in this instance shared by both Weber and Walsh may indeed indicate a connection between them.

Weber was almost certainly the first piano-maker in Ireland, and contemporary with the earliest makers of the instrument in England: an entry in his ledger for Mrs. David Latouche records a sum due for tuning her 'Forte Piano' from 17th October 1765.

Only one pianoforte definitely attributable to Weber is presently recorded. Dated 1774, it was photographed in 1902. Its external appearance suggests it to have been a Zumpe-style instrument.

Provenance
1997 Purchased at Sotheby's auction rooms.

TECHNICAL DATA

Date	1780
Nameboard Inscription	
	FERDINAND WEBER fecit
Soundboard Inscription	
	Ferdinand Weber fecit Dublin 1780
Compass	5 Octaves, G_1-g^3.
	Ivory Naturals. Ebony capped sharps.
3-Octave-span	491
Registration	1x8'. One row of jacks.

	G_1	c^2	g^3
Scaling	1648	327	118
Pluck-point	191	75	44
Gauges 1996	0.71	0.34	0.33
Gauges Marked	11	4	4

Case	Mahogany veneered oak.
	Length 2046. Width 750. Depth 216.
Restorations	Restoration to working order in 1998-9 by Miles Hellon.

10. PIANOFORTE in the form of a half-moon table by William Southwell, Dublin, c. 1782. Cabinet work attributed to William Moore.

The property of Mr. Alec Cobbe.

One of the characteristics exhibited by William Southwell's work throughout his spectacular career is a flair for decoration. Few pianofortes of the eighteenth century are as elegant and decorative as his metamorphic half-moon tables, a form that was highly fashionable in Dublin at the time.

Southwell was born in Dublin and apprenticed to Ferdinand Weber with whom he remained until 1782. In this year he set up his workshop in Marlborough Street, and the half-moon table pianos must have been amongst his earliest independent productions. About six have survived, all bearing Southwell's name.

William Moore, after working for Mayhew & Ince in London, set up in Dublin around 1782, the year Southwell also set up independently. Moore became celebrated for his inlaid halfmoon tables and his name has therefore been linked to Southwell's in these half-moon table instruments. Evidence substantiating a connection is found in Dublin directories dating after Southwell's move to London when Moore advertised himself as 'Cabinet and Piano-forte-maker'.

Perhaps the most interesting feature of the instrument is its action, which is of a German type with the hammer mounted in a *kapsel* and pointing towards the player. That the action is of a South German type, rather than the kind used in Saxony by Gottfried Silbermann, suggests that Southwell was either well versed by his master in all German actions or had travelled to Germany himself. No use of German action is found in instruments by any other makers in Britain or Ireland.

The damping system however is completely novel. On all English early square pianos, mahogany dampers are made to bear on the strings from above by means of whalebone springs. Southwell constructed an overdamper in lead, shaped and engraved to resemble a peacock complete with eye, beak and plumage, where the weight produces a particularly effective damping action. This idea was later used by Broadwood but as an underdamper. (see No. 20).

These highly ornamental instruments were clearly commissioned by or aimed at patrons of very considerable means: Clinkscale has reported that the Duchess of Grafton in Dublin possessed two of them, to be played *à deux* by her children.

Provenance
1995 Purchased from Alan Rubin.

TECHNICAL DATA

Date	c. 1782
Nameboard Inscription	
	SOUTHWELL
Compass	5 Octaves, F_1/G_1 - f^3.
	Ivory naturals. Ebony capped sharps.
3-Octave-span	487.
Stringing	Bichord throughout.
Scaling	Not original.
Action	*Prellmechanik* with 'peacock' overdampers throughout.
Stops	One knee-lever controlling Venetian swell and dampers.
Case	Pine, veneered with satinwood and thuya. Length 1574. Width 592. Depth 168.
Restorations	Restored to working order in 1999.

10.3 Inlay work attributed to William Moore, of Dublin.

10.4 Interior of the instrument.

10.1 Half moon table piano by William Southwell, c.1782, closed.

10.2 The instrument, opened.

11. CLAVICHORD
by Christian Gotthelf Hoffmann, Ronneburg, Saxony, 1784.

The clavichord has the simplest possible action of any keyboard instrument. The sound is produced only while a metal tangent attached to the inner end of the key lever is in contact with the string. The note can be made to waver in pitch by vibrating the key whilst it is depressed. The resulting 'vibrato', known in Germany as *Bebung*, is, among keyboard instruments, unique to the clavichord. The instrument is quiet in its loudest moments; it is however, capable of rendering, in miniature, loud and soft playing and this coupled with the 'vibrato' makes it immensely expressive and intimate.

These qualities have not been lost on composers. It is said that the instrument was the favourite of Johann Sebastian Bach on account of its singing tone. This was according to his son Carl Philipp Emmanuel, himself a devotee and noted performer on the clavichord. Carl Philipp Emmanuel owned a clavichord to which he was famously attached, made by his father's friend and keyboard instrument maker Gottfreid Silvermann. Another maker favoured by C.P.E. Bach was Christian Gottlob Friederici of Gera, Saxony. This Hoffmann clavichord closely resembles the latter's instruments. Ronneburg is situated within a mile or two of Gera, which may point to a connection. The clavichord reached a zenith of popularity in eighteenth-century Germany. Mozart's wife recorded that he composed *La Clemenza di Tito*, *The Magic Flute*, and the *Requiem* on his clavichord which survives in the Geburtshaus museum in Salzburg. Few French or Italian examples and only one English are known.

Little is known of Christian Gotthelf Hoffmann. He may have been related to the Christian Hoffmann who made violins at Dresden and at least one keyboard instrument which he bequeathed to his friend Johann Sebastian Bach. Two clavichords by Christian Gotthelf Hoffmann are extant.

11.1 Clavichord by Christian Gotthelf Hoffmann.

11.2 Inscription on reverse of nameboard.

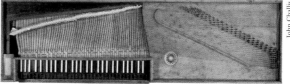

11.3 The instrument seen from above.

11.4 Detail of the rose.

Provenance
Broadwood Collection.
c. 1970 Purchased by Michael Thomas.
1981 Purchased from him by Alec Cobbe.
1983 Exhibited The Fitzwilliam Museum, Cambridge,
A Century of Keyboard Instruments, No. 3.
1997 Given to The Cobbe Collection Trust.

TECHNICAL DATA

Date	1784
Serial Number	32
Nameboard Inscription	
(On reverse)	S.D.G.
	Christian Gotthelf Hoffmann
	in Ronneburg. Nom: 32
	1784
Paper label	Repariert v. H Seyffarth
on belly rail	Leipzig Gohlis 1904
	Instrumentenmacher
Compass	5 Octaves, F_1-f^3. Ebony naturals. Ivory-capped sharps.
3-Octave span	485
Stringing	Bichord throughout.

	F_1	c^2	f^3
Scaling	1440	254	94
Gauges	Spun	0.33	0.25

Action	Unfretted.
Case	Oak. Length 1738. Width 490. Depth 154.
Restorations	Restored to working order by P Bavington in 1998.

12. SQUARE PIANOFORTE
by Sébastian Erard, Paris, 1787.
Reputedly made for Queen Marie Antoinette.
The gift of Renée, Lady Iliffe and Mr. Alec Cobbe

Sébastian Erard was born in Alsace and became one of the earliest piano-makers in Paris, his first pianofortes being made around 1777. Those that survive are closely based on the Zumpes that were being imported in large numbers from London.

He received the encouragement of the musical Queen Marie Antoinette, who had as Dauphine received the dedication by the composer Nicolas Joseph Hüllmandel of France's first printed piano music. The extent of her patronage is shown by the fact that when Erard was imprisoned in 1785 for flouting the complex Parisian guild rules in relation to the cabinet work in his instruments, the King and Queen intervened personally and granted him a special *privilege* to make his own cases. During the Revolution Erard's Royalist connections made it absolutely necessary for him to flee to England, and in London he wasted no time in setting up a second workshop whilst his brother looked after the Paris establishment. The two workshops produced pianos in tandem for a century.

Although the instrument adopts the form and action of Zumpe's instruments, in one respect Erard made a significant improvement over the English models. In Zumpe's and most other English instruments the dampers and buff mechanism were operated by handstops at the left hand side. This rendered modification by stop-changing whilst both hands were playing impossible: Erard overcame this by simply substituting Viennese-style knee-levers to operate the stops.

Erard's genius, supported by a brilliant business sense, was to make him a very rich man. After the Revolution he acquired and installed his family in one of Marie Antoinette's residences, Château de la Muette, and assembled a large collection of paintings which included works attributed to Raphael, Titian, and Correggio. There was also, not surprisingly, a collection

John Challis

12.1 Square pianoforte by Sébastian Erard, 1787, made for Marie Antoinette.

12.2 Detail of the keyboard.

of musical instruments of which the present pianoforte was the star piece. For nearly thirty years of Erard's long life his nephew Pierre was partner and helpmate in his great invention, the double escapement action that forms the basis of that in modern instruments. Pierre's wife, an Erard cousin, lent the instrument to a number of exhibitions both in France and England as a chef d'œuvre made by their uncle for the Queen and re-purchased in the revolutionary sales. After her death

12.3 Detail of the nameboard.

12.4 Inscription on the soundboard.

at the end of the nineteenth century, there being no Erard children, the family firm was inherited by a cousin, M. de Francheville who took no interest in it. Marie Antoinette's piano was sold in 1903 for thirty thousand francs to William Waldorf Astor who placed it in his drawing room at Hever Castle, Kent. The instrument survived a major flood there c.1968 when it was submerged for several hours.

Provenance
By repute made for Queen Marie Antoinette.
According to Erard tradition re-purchased by Sébastian Erard in the revolutionary sales.
1872 Exhibited The South Kensington Museum, London, Ancient Musical Instruments, No. 40, lent by Madame Erard.
1900 Exhibited l'Exposition Centennale et Rétrospective, Paris. No. 144.
c.1906 Sold by Erards to William Waldorf Astor Ff 30,000.
In Lord Astor's typescript inventory of Hever (undated) p. 59, ' Trianon - 30,000frs - Marie Antoinette piano. Sold to me by Erard by whom it was made 1779 (sic)'
(The date given is that of the Erard harpsichord also purchased by Lord Astor.)
1971 Sold by Lord Astor of Hever, Christie's 15th July Lot 68, 1100 Gns. Bought Frank Berendt.
In correspondence between Lord Astor's grandson and Mr Berendt another document from the Astor archives was cited

'My records show that my Grandfather acquired it in Paris in 1906 and a contemporary inventory describes it as follows: "1906. Bought of F. Robert (Lacade) a Spinet or old pianoforte by Erard in Spanish mahogany case with brass moulding and chased beading 5' wide (made for Queen Marie Antoinette and re-purchased by Erard from Trianon after the Revolution)".

1983 Purchased from Frank Berendt by Renée, Lady Iliffe and Alec Cobbe.

1983 Exhibited The Fitzwilliam Museum, Cambridge, *A Century of Keyboard Instruments*, No. 6.

1997 Given to The Cobbe Collection Trust.

12.5 Label on underside of piano.

TECHNICAL DATA

Date	1787
Nameboard Inscription	
	Sebastianus Erard Parisiis
	1787
	Rue du Mail No 37.
Soundboard Inscription	
	Sebastien Erard a Paris 1786
Inscription on bottom keylever	
	Joints le 24 Mars 1834
	A.C.
	V. Potter 14 April 1960
	Hever Castle
Label on Baseboard	
	HISTOIRE DU TRAVAIL
	Section II Musique
	Piano de La reine Marie Antoinette
	de Sébastien Erard 1787
	Collection Erard
Compass	5 Octaves, F_1-f^3.
	Ivory naturals and ebony sharps.
	(Replacements).
3-Octave span	488
Stringing	Bichord throughout.

12.6 Queen Marie Antoinette at the keyboard.

	F_1	c^2	f^3
Scaling	1300	286	102
Strike point	77	24	17
Gauges	Spun	0.44	0.36

Action	English single (Zumpe's first action).
	Overdampers throughout.
	Overlaid passive soundboard.
Stops	2 Knee-levers:
	Dampers.
	Buff.
Case	Mahogany veneered on mahogany.
	Length 1480. Width 557. Depth 200.
Restorations	Restored to working order in 1984.

13. DOUBLE MANUAL HARPSICHORD

by Burkat Shudi and John Broadwood, London, 1787.

The property of The Royal Academy of Music, on permanent loan to The Cobbe Collection Trust.

C. Barda, London

13.1 Double manual harpsichord by Burkat Shudi, 1787.

In 1728 Burkat Shudi established a harpsichord business in London that thrived as one of the two leading practices in the capital for the rest of the century. Handel patronised the firm in 1729, making a gift of a Shudi harpsichord to the soprano Anna Strada. Shudi also made an instrument for Frederick, Prince of Wales in the 1720's. In 1769 John Broadwood married Shudi's daughter and became a partner in the business, which continued firstly as Burkat Shudi and John Broadwood, and subsequently as John Broadwood and Sons until 1970. This has been the longest continuously running firm of instrument-makers, the duration exceeding that of the Ruckers dynasty by over a century.

Shudi, having achieved all possible success in London, courted recognition in continental Europe by presenting an immensely grand harpsichord to the famously musical King, Frederick the Great in 1744. He proudly had himself and his family painted in a conversation piece around it before its despatch. The instrument itself does not seem to have survived, but it was probably shown to Johann Sebastian Bach on his visit to the King in 1747. Shudi's gesture was ultimately rewarded by an order in 1765 from Frederick the Great for no less than four harpsichords, one of which was played in London by the nine-year-old Mozart before being sent.

These latter instruments for King Frederick were all fitted with Shudi's special invention, a shuttered internal swell mechanism resembling a venetian blind, resulting in its name 'Venetian swell'. By means of a pedal, this gives the instrument rudimentary capabilities of crescendo and diminuendo. The invention was patented in 1769, the year John Broadwood's name started to appear on the nameboards of the harpsichords. It may well have been Shudi's attempt to combat a perceived threat to the harpsichord posed by the pianofortes then appearing in London. It can be seen in this instrument.

Provenance
1938 Bought by Captain Evelyn Broadwood at Puttick and Simpson (vendor not recorded).
At the Broadwood house at Lyne till 1975.
1989 Given to The Royal Academy of Music by The Broadwood Trust.
1991 Exhibited The British Library, London,
Mozart: 'Prodigy of Nature'.
1992 Transferred on permanent loan to the Cobbe Collection.

TECHNICAL DATA

Date	1787
Serial Number	1076
Nameboard Inscription	
	Burkat Shudi et Johannes Broadwood.
	Patent No 1076, Londini Fecerunt 1787.
	Great Pulteney Street, Golden Square
Compass	5 Octaves, F_1-f^3. Double manual.
	Ivory Naturals. Ebony sharps.
3-Octave span	489.
Registration	2x8', 1x4' and Lute. 4 rows of jacks.

	F_1	c^2	f^3
8' Scaling	1846/1832	345/327	131/124
			Long 8'/Short 8'
Pluck point	210/228	94/109	56/71
Gauges (1991)	0.7	0.23	0.23
4' Scaling	1052	166	64
Pluck point	138	66	46

Stops	5 Handstops, 2 Pedals.	
	Handstops:	Pedals:
	Machine	Machine
	Lute	Venetian swell
	4'	
	Buff	
	Front 8'	
	Back 8'	
Case	Mahogany veneered on oak.	
	Length 2449. Width 958. Depth 320.	
Restorations	By A Chappell before acquisition.	

14. GRAND PIANOFORTE
by Crang Hancock, London, c. 1790.
With a silver plaque engraved 'Warranted by Mr Dibdin'.

Purchased by Alec Cobbe with a grant from the Manifold trust, and given to the Cobbe Collection Trust

Charles Dibdin (1745–1814) was an energetic composer of songs and pieces for the theatre. His use of 'a new instrument called piano forte' to accompany a song in Covent Garden Theatre in 1767 is thought to be the earliest recorded public appearance of the instrument in England. (For the first public use as a solo instrument see No. 6). He later achieved celebrity as a public entertainer using a piano by Crang Hancock augmented with an organ and other effects to create a one-man-band. Dibdin's career was erratic and he was forced to leave the country on at least one occasion because of debts.

At a sale of Dibdin's effects in 1805 the 'curious and entertaining instrument with which Mr D. accompanied his songs' was purchased by a Dr. W. Kitchiner. In 1823, Kitchiner published a biographical memoir of Dibdin in which he gives the following description of his purchase:

It was a Grand Piano-forte with Two Strings, made by Crang Hancock, which was laid upon an Organ built by the same Artist, and was very sensibly constructed with a fine full-toned *Stop Diapason*, a powerful *Principal*, and an excellent *Trumpet*. This Organ is now in Winslade Church, in the County of Southampton.

Some of the pipes of the Trumpet were occasionally removed to introduce others which imitated the grunting of a Pig, which Mr D. employed in his Song of the Learned Pig; and others which imitated the Ba-a of Sheep, and the bleating of a calf. There was also a set of BELLS, which, by drawing a stop, were acted on by the Keys of the Piano-forte; and all these could be played either separately or, by a coupling movement, all together. Near his right foot was placed a SIDE DRUM with four hammers, acted upon with one Pedal, (the principal Stop of the Organ imitating THE FIFE,) and a TAMBOURINE with one Pedal, which produced at

14.1 Detail of nameboard, showing silver plaque.

one stroke, the jingling and beat of the Tambourine with very good effect, and which he used more frequently than any of the other auxiliaries. Near his left foot was placed a small CHINESE GONG, which we do not remember that he made any use of, except in that part of the Song of *The Watchman* when he said, "St. Paul's strikes ONE!"......(he) occasionally accompanied himself in his singing with the Stop Diapason coupled to the Piano; which had an excellent effect, but it was extremely difficult to keep the Strings of the latter in exact tune with the Pipes of the former.

The elegant silver plaque on this instrument most likely betokens a promotional arrangement between the composer and Crang Hancock. Several of Dibdin's songs remained popular throughout the nineteenth century and in 1860 he was acknowledged in the first history in English of the pianoforte, by Edward Rimbault. The work was dedicated to Henry Dibdin because 'to his grandfather is due the merit of having first introduced the pianoforte to public notice in England'.

Provenance
1996 Christie's 12th June Lot 1, purchased by Alec Cobbe.
1997 Given to The Cobbe Collection Trust.

TECHNICAL DATA

Date	c. 1790
Nameboard Inscription	
	By Royal Patent Crang Hancock London
Plaque Inscription	Warranted by Mr Dibdin
Compass	5 Octaves, F_1-f^3.
	Ivory naturals. Ebony sharps.
3-Octave-span	487
Stringing	Bichord throughout. Undivided bridge.

	F_1	c^2	f^3
Scaling	1415	284	112 (Longest)
Strike-point	160	29	20
Gauges	Twisted	0.4	0.4

Action	Reversed English Grand. Overdampers throughout.
Stops	1 pedal: Harp.
Case	Mahogany and satinwood veneered on oak. Length 1846. Width 926. Depth 214.
Restorations	Acquired with collapsed soundboard, 1999. Returned to playing order by David Hunt.

Restored to playing order with the assistance of a grant from The Rt. Hon. The Baroness Thatcher, L.G., O.M., F.R.S.

14.2 Grand pianoforte by Crang Hancock, c.1790.

15. GRAND PIANOFORTE
by a pupil of Johann Andreas Stein, South Germany or Vienna, last quarter of the eighteenth century.

Johann Andreas Stein can be regarded as the brilliant inventor of a type of pianoforte which dominated the writing for the instrument in Vienna from the 1770's for over half a century. This pianoforte is closely based on Stein's later products both in action and construction. Stein's success stemmed from his invention of an escapement for a previously somewhat primitive German action known as *'prellmechanik'* which may not have been used in 'grand' instruments prior to Stein. In his action, unlike that of Cristofori or Silbermann, the hammer is attached to the key lever, mounted in a *'Kapsel'*, and points towards the player. Stein's escapement rendered the action very responsive. Of this device Mozart wrote :

15.1 Grand pianoforte by a pupil of Johannes Stein, last quarter of the 18th century.

His [Stein's] instruments have this special advantage over others that they are made with escape action. Only one maker in a hundred bothers about this. But without an escapement it is impossible to avoid jangling and vibration after the note is struck. When you touch the keys, the hammers fall back again the moment after they have struck the strings, whether you hold the keys or release them.

Chief amongst Stein's pupils was his own daughter, Nannette, who began helping her father at eight years old, her age when Mozart stayed with the Stein family in 1777. In another letter to his father he described her playing in detail, for she was judged even by Mozart to possess a great talent in music. However Mozart was most enthusiastic of all about Stein's pianofortes, judging them to be the best he had ever encountered. The greater part of the long letter to his father, from which the extract above is quoted, is devoted to a description of their construction and qualities, the only instance in Mozart's writings to give an insight into his views on the pianoforte. He was to use and recommend Stein instruments for the remainder of his life.

Stein died in 1792, and his daughter continued the

business, moving to Vienna in 1793, firstly in partnership with her brother, and after her marriage to Andreas Streicher independently, describing herself as Nannette Streicher née Stein. She became one of Vienna's most important figures (see No. 27) and is the only woman maker to have achieved prominence in this field. In 1801 she took the eminently practical step of publishing a manual to accompany her instruments, giving hints and instructions on maintenance, tuning and playing. This instrument and its action tally so exactly with her diagrams illustrating this publication, that it may indeed have been made by her.

Viennese or German pianofortes did not at first have pedals, and the dampers on this instrument are raised by means of a knee lever under the keyboard; a second knee-lever operates the 'moderator', which mutes the sound by interposing a series of leather tongues under the strings so that the hammers strike the strings through the tongues; and a third operates a 'Turkish stop' which lowers a strip of parchment to touch lightly on the bass strings to give a buzzing effect. The use of this was specifically indicated by Mozart in a single instance, the final Rondo of Sonata K.331 marked *Alla Turca*.

15.2 The instrument seen from above.

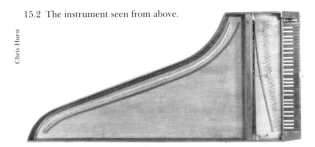

Chris Hurst

Chris Hurst

15.3 Detail of the underside, showing the kneelevers at the front of the instrument.

Mozart refers to the knee-levers of Stein's pianos:

the device you work with your knee is better than on other instruments. I have only to touch it and it works; and when you shift your knee the slightest bit, you do not hear the least reverberation.

This is of particular interest to pianists since most of Stein's instruments were not made with Turkish or moderator stops and it therefore suggests that Mozart expected to use the sustaining device as a matter of course.

Provenance
1978 acquired by Alec Cobbe from the restoration workshop of Herr Watzek, Vienna (prior to restoration), through Dr. Otmar Seemann.
1983 Exhibited The Fitzwilliam Museum, Cambridge,

A Century of Keyboard Instruments, No. 5.
1991 Exhibited The British Library, London *Mozart: 'Prodigy of Nature'*.
1997 Given to The Cobbe Collection Trust.

TECHNICAL DATA

Maker	Attributed to a pupil of Johann Andreas Stein.
Date	c. 1785-95.
Nameboard Inscription	
	Indecipherable.
Compass	5 Octaves, F_1-f^3.
	Ebony naturals. Bone-capped sharps.
3-Octave span	463
Stringing	Bichord throughout.

	F_1	c^2	f^3
Scaling	1748	279	115
Strike point	137	31	13
Gauges	0.95	0.44	0.40

Action	German - Stein type, with escapement but no check.
	Overdampers throughout.
Stops	3 Knee-levers:
	Bassoon
	Dampers
	Moderator.
Case	Mahogany veneered on cherry and pine.
	Length 2120. Width 933. Depth 230.
Restorations	Restored to working order in 1983.

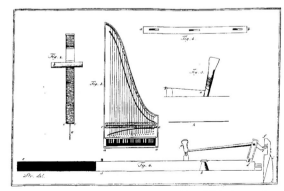

15.4 Working diagram from Nannette Stein's published manual.

16. SQUARE PIANOFORTE
by Longman and Broderip, London, c.1791.

Longman and Broderip were one of the chief musical houses in late eighteenth century London. They published music and sold musical instruments of many kinds. They were the London agents for the Viennese publishers, Artaria, who were Haydn's and Mozart's main publishers. It is unlikely that they were the actual manufacturers of the instruments they sold but rather contracted with diverse makers to place their name on the instruments that were to be supplied to them.

This would seem to be the case with two makers who at different times achieved significant advances in square piano design. One of these was John Geib who in 1786 invented and patented an escapement for the square piano action. This made it both more sensitive and easier to regulate. Longman & Broderip formed a contract with him so that all instruments with this improvement would effectively be sold through them. As a result of Geib's patent, the improvement did not become available to other makers until around 1800, when it was generally adopted by all. This instrument incorporates a development of Geib's escapement action. Another maker with whom the firm appear to have contracted was William Southwell (see No. 17). The firm was bankrupted around 1798, when it was rescued by Muzio Clementi and continued under his name.

Provenance
Purchased by Alec Cobbe.
1997 Given to the Cobbe Collection Trust.

TECHNICAL DATA

Date	c. 1791
Serial Number	2001
Nameboard	BY ROYAL PATENT
Inscription	LONGMAN & BRODERIP
	MUSICAL INSTRUMENT MAKERS
	No 26 CHEAPSIDE & No 13 HAYMARKET
	LONDON

David Mees

16.1 Square piano by Longman and Broderip, c. 1792.

Compass	5 Octaves, F_1-f^3.
	Ivory naturals. Ebony sharps.
3-Octave span	482.
Stringing	Bichord throughout.

	F_1	c^2	f^3
Scaling	1380	300	112
Strike point	104	27	17

Action	L&B patent single escapement - no check.
	Overdampers throughout.
	Overlaid passive soundboard missing.
Stops	3 Hand-stops:
	Two for divided dampers.
	Buff.
Case	Solid mahogany.
	Length 1556. Width 551. Depth 225.
Restorations	Awaiting restoration.

17. SQUARE PIANOFORTE

by William Southwell, Dublin, c. 1793-4.

The property of Mr. Alec Cobbe.

The compass for most keyboard instruments across Europe for the greater part of the eighteenth century was five octaves. Mozart (d. 1791) exceeded it in only one of his works. In England in 1789, Jan Ladislav Dussek had pressed Broadwood to make grand pianos with a compass extended in the treble to five-and-a-half octaves, and these went into general production quite quickly. Beethoven would have been well aware of the expansion (he would have seen it on Haydn's Longman & Broderip in 1795 and on Viennese pianos appearing with one or two extra notes in the late 1790s), but was relatively conservative in this respect, and only moved outside five octaves in his writing as late as 1799.

To increase the compass of a grand piano does not pose any great technical problems beyond that of making the instrument correspondingly wider, and the frame strong enough to withstand the extra tension. In square pianos, which comprised the vast majority of pianos sold by any maker, there is a substantial obstacle in that the length of the instrument is the sum total of both that of the keyboard and the soundboard. The expansion of the keyboard would seem to result in an instrument that would either be so long that it would lose its advantage over a grand pianoforte, as well as being impractical for tuning, or else to be at the expense of the soundboard which would greatly impair the sound.

The problem was brilliantly solved by Southwell who had the idea of running the extra treble keys under the soundboard, with the hammers rising through a narrow gap at the back of the soundboard to strike the strings. In this way there was no loss of tone through a diminishment of soundboard area. Southwell's discovery was of considerable commercial significance, and after patenting his idea in 1794 he opened a workshop in London to reap the potential rewards. In fact these seem to have come from a contract with

Longman & Broderip who were advertising this new improved pianoforte 'with the additional notes' shortly after Southwell's arrival in London in the same year.

This instrument was made in Southwell's Dublin workshop and the nameboard mentions the patent, granted or perhaps pending. The lid of the case which matches the rest perfectly in its veneer and marquetry

17.1 Square pianoforte by William Southwell, c. 1793-4.

17.2 Detail of keywell showing nameboard decoration.

decorations, was however made in the first instance for a five octave instrument. This can be seen by the two front lid-flaps which normally open separately but here have been fixed together during the construction of the instrument to open as one. The join which should correspond with the treble end of the keywell occurs at the extent of a five rather than the five and a half octave keywell. The instrument is probably, therefore, one of Southwell's earliest five-and-a-half octave productions.

Provenance
Purchased by Ian Pleeth at auction in the West country. Bought from him by Alec Cobbe.

TECHNICAL DATA

Date	c. 1793/4
Serial Number	1617
Nameboard Inscription	
	PATENT FORTE PIANO
	(No) 1617
	Wm Southwell Dublin
Compass	5 Octaves and a fifth, F_1/G_1 - c^4.
	Ivory naturals. Ebony capped sharps.
3-Octave-span	489
Stringing	Bichord throughout.

	F_1	c^2	c^4
Scaling	1349	303	82
Strike-point	124	37	17
Gauges	Spun	0.44	0.40

Action	English single. Overdampers to c^3.
	Overlaid passive soundboard
	(reconstruction).
Stops	2 Knee-levers:
	Buff.
	(Venetian) Swell (missing).
Case	Mahogany veneered mahogany.
	Length 1546. Width 535. Depth 216.
Restorations	Restored to working order by David Hunt
	in 1989.

Chris Hurst

17.3 Detail showing fretwork with the Irish harp within the instrument.

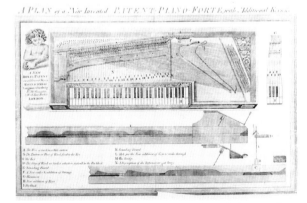

17.4 Engraved advertisement of Longman and Broderip promoting Southwell's invention.

18. SQUARE PIANOFORTE
by John Bland, London, 1794.

The property of Mr. Alec Cobbe.

John Bland was a music publisher who changed musical history when he invited Haydn to travel to London. Haydn spent his first night in London at Bland's house. As well as selling music and instruments which he certainly did not make himself, Bland marketed portrait prints of composers, the original paintings of which hung in his shop. It was Bland who commissioned, in the same year as this instrument was made, the famous portrait of Haydn painted by Thomas Hardy now in the collection of The Royal College of Music. There is an anecdote that before Haydn's visit to England the composer had swapped with Bland the manuscript of a string quartet for some English razors. The work was dubbed 'The Razor Quartet' and H.C. Robbins Landon has discovered some evidence in support of the tale, in a letter from Haydn to Bland acknowledging receipt of razors. A number of square pianofortes bearing Bland's name have survived, exhibiting more or less similar characteristics, and there has been some debate as to the identity of their maker.

Provenance
Purchased privately by Ian Pleeth.
Bought from him by Alec Cobbe.

TECHNICAL DATA

Date	1794		
Nameboard Inscription			
	John Bland, No 45 Holborn, London, 1794		
Compass	5 Octaves, F_1-f^3.		
	Ivory Naturals. Ebony sharps.		
3-Octave-span	485.		
Stringing	Bichord throughout.		

	F_1	c^2	f^3
Scaling	1392	303	111
Strike-point	92	37	20
Gauges	Spun	0.4	0.36

Action	English single . Overdampers throughout. Overlaid passive soundboard.
Stops	1 handstop: Dampers. 1 pedal: Lid swell.
Case	Solid mahogany. Length 1563. Width 532. Depth 200.
Restorations	Restored to working order by David Hunt in 1996.

David Mees

18.1 Square piano by John Bland, 1794.

19. GRAND PIANOFORTE
by Longman & Broderip, London, c. 1795.

Whilst square pianos by Longman & Broderip survive in considerable numbers, very few of their grand pianofortes are extant, this example being one of perhaps only three. Of the others, one is the instrument taken to Vienna from London by Haydn in 1795. H.C. Robbins Landon has suggested that as Longman and Broderip were facing some financial difficulties around this time, the pianoforte may have been offered to the composer as part payment of commission fees for music that they had published. It is clear from detailed constructional comparison that both Haydn's and the present instrument were made by the same maker, and there are indications to suggest that this may have been William Southwell from Dublin (see No. 17) with whom Longman & Broderip were evidently and recently connected.

In common with other English grand pianofortes of the time, the instrument has two pedals; that on the right sustains the dampers, whilst on the left is the *una corda* pedal which slides the movement so that the hammers may hit three, two or only one of the three strings of each note. This device was not employed on Viennese pianofortes of the time where softening of tone was achieved by a moderator stop (see No. 15). The English action had also evolved differently from that in Vienna; the former being characterised by a sonorous strength with depth and heaviness of touch and ponderous damping, the latter by a lightness of touch and neatness of sound with very precise damping. The English instrument was capable of a much larger sound overall, and the somewhat indistinct damping results in a wash of sound that presages the romantic era.

Haydn's dramatic musical reaction to the larger sound of the English piano can be readily appreciated by a simple visual comparison of the score of the opening passage of Sonata in E♭ HOB XVI/52 composed in London with similar passages in his previous piano works. Beethoven, who had recently been Haydn's

Courtesy of Sotheby's

19.1 Grand pianoforte by Longman and Broderip, c.1795.

Chris Hurst

19.2 Detail of keywell and nameboard decoration.

19.3 Detail of ornamental fretwork within the instrument.

TECHNICAL DATA

Date	c.1795
Serial Number	38?
Nameboard Inscription	

By Royal Patent
Longman & Broderip
Musical Instrument Makers
No 26 Cheapside & No 13 Haymarket
LONDON

Inscription	'OA' stamped in plank.
Compass	5 Octaves and a fifth, F_1-c^4.
	Ivory naturals. Ebony sharps.
3-Octave-span	488.
Stringing	Trichord throughout. Bridge divided at A/A#.

	F_1	c^2	c^4
Scaling	1708	286	77
Strike-point	169	22	5.5
Gauges	0.8	0.48	0.40

Action	English Grand - with backchecks.
	Overdampers throughout.
Stops	2 Pedals and 1 Handstop:
	Keyboard shift pedal with *unacorda* handstop.
	Dampers.
Case	Mahogany veneered on oak.
	Length 2293. Width 1049. Depth 300.
Restorations	Restoration work by David Hunt in 1994 and 1996.

Restored to playing order with the assistance of a grant from Sarasin Investment Management Ltd.

pupil, experienced the London pianoforte at the master's house. He was particularly excited by the *una corda* device which he later attempted to have the Viennese maker Anton Walter incorporate into a new instrument. Haydn's Longman & Broderip almost certainly saw the first exposition by Beethoven of the three earliest piano sonatas, Opus 2, dedicated to his teacher, and the instrument would appear to have sparked in Beethoven a lifelong love affair with all things English.

Provenance
1972 Sotheby's 21st December,
purchased by John and Mary Best
1993 Sotheby's 18th November Lot 172,
purchased by Alec Cobbe.
1997 Given to The Cobbe Collection Trust.

20. SQUARE PIANOFORTE
by John Broadwood and Son, London, 1795.
The property of Mr. Alec Cobbe.

This model, somewhat basic in that it has no handstops or music rest inside the instrument, nonetheless represents the fruits of John Broadwood's untiring efforts and researches to improve the efficiency and stability of the square piano. The most drastic improvement is the removal of the wrest pins from the treble end, where they would normally emerge from a plank placed at a diagonal under the soundboard, to the back of the instrument where there is an altogether more solid construction to withstand strain.

The instrument is also furnished with a counterbalanced brass underdamping system which works extremely efficiently and makes for almost Viennese style precise damping. These dampers have traditionally been referred to as 'peacock dampers' though unlike the dampers so termed in Southwell's half-moon table instruments (see No. 10), the silhouette of the brass piece bears no resemblance to the bird. The use of this name suggests that Broadwood probably borrowed the whole idea from Southwell, but reversed it from an over- to an under-damping system. It is rather superior to some of the damping systems which followed, but was probably abandoned owing to the expense of manufacture.

Provenance
c.1978 Purchased from Don Adcock, Suffolk.

TECHNICAL DATA

Date	1795
Serial Number	3168
Nameboard Inscription	

John Broadwood and Son
Great Pulteney Street Golden Square
Patent London 1795

Compass	5 Octaves, F_1-f^3.
	Ivory naturals. Ebony sharps.
3-Octave span	490.
Stringing	Bichord throughout.

	F_1	c^2	f^3
Scaling	1355	281	110
Strike point	86	30	22
Gauges	Spun	0.4	0.4

Action	English single. Underdampers throughout. Overlaid passive soundboard missing.
Case	Solid mahogany. Length 1568. Width 527. Depth 225.
Restorations	Restored to working order by David Hunt in 1992.

Chris Hurst

20.1 Square pianoforte by John Broadwood, 1795.

21. GRAND PIANOFORTE
by John Broadwood and Son, London, 1807.

The property of the Royal Academy of Music, on permanent loan to the Cobbe Collection Trust.

John Broadwood devoted his earliest endeavours in pianoforte-manufacturing to improving and producing square pianofortes. He did not turn his attention to grand pianofortes until the mid 1780s. The action in his grand pianos was based on the work of Americus Backers, who had developed a grand piano action, deriving from Cristofori's original invention, in the 1760s and 1770s. Broadwood quickly gained a supremacy in the field and Dussek gave his instruments prominence in public performance during his London years, 1789-1799. Dussek also lent his Broadwood instrument to Haydn following the latter's arrival in London. The present instrument, a normal model in musical respects, has been expensively finished and fitted with a handsome stand with lyre-shaped supports.

C. Barda, London

21.1 Grand pianoforte by Broadwood & Sons, 1807.

Provenance
Entry in the Broadwood ledgers
'Thursday 5th November 1807
GFP add ORN^d. 3 Pedals, Lyre Frame No 3992 delivered at Mr Warner's, Crescent, Blackheath. Clerk   Warner £80.'
1989 Given to The Royal Academy of Music by the Broadwood Trust.
1992 Transferred on permanent loan to The Cobbe Collection.

TECHNICAL DATA

Date	1807
Serial Number	3992
Nameboard Inscription	1807

John Broadwood & Son
Makers to His Majesty
and the Princesses
Great Pulteney Street, Golden Square,
London.

Compass   5 Octaves and a fifth, F_1-c^4.

	Ivory Naturals. Ebony Sharps
3-Octave span	489.
Stringing	Trichord throughout. Bridge divided at $G^{\#}$/A.

	F_1	c^2	c^4
Scaling	1725	275	75
Strike point	167	28	4
Gauges (1991)	0.70	0.48	0.44

Action	English grand - with backchecks. Overdampers throughout.
Stops	3 Pedals and 1 Hand-stop:
	Keyboard shift pedal with
	una corda handstop
	Dampers bass
	Dampers treble.
Case	Mahogany veneered on oak. Length 2245. Width 1051. Depth 294.
Restorations	Restored by T. Chappell prior to acquisition

22. GRAND PIANOFORTE

by Anton Walter and Son, Vienna, c.1815.

Acquired by The Cobbe Collection Trust using funds donated by Alec Cobbe.

Anton Walter was an important Viennese pianoforte-maker during the last quarter of the eighteenth century and the first quarter of the nineteenth. He was commissioned by Mozart to make a pianoforte in 1784. This was, presumably the instrument referred to by Leopold Mozart in a letter to his daughter, written in 1785 whilst staying with his son in Vienna:

'It is impossible for me to describe the rush and bustle. Since my arrival your brother's fortepiano has been taken at least a dozen times to the theatre or some other house'.

It survives today in the Mozart Geburtshaus Museum in Salzburg.

The patronage of Mozart would have made Walter's reputation. By the end of the century Walter clearly considered himself pre-eminent in his field, for when he received an indirect request from Beethoven in 1801 to make a pianoforte incorporating the English *una corda* device, then unknown on Viennese instruments, he simply refused. Another famous instrument by this maker, a square pianoforte, was made for Schubert's friend August Rieder, the painter. Rieder had commissioned it in order that Schubert, who was unable to afford an up-to-date instrument, could visit whenever he wished to play. His portrait of Schubert shows the composer seated beside it, and it survives today in the Kunsthistorisches Museum, Vienna. Walter's stepson joined him in the business around 1800 but pre-deceased him.

This very ornamental instrument, the case veneered in an exotic Hungarian ash, is an excellent specimen of the Viennese cabinet-maker's art. It is, if not the only, one of the very few full-sized instruments by Walter in England today and it possesses what had by this date become the usual gamut of pedals in Vienna, sustaining, moderator, bassoon or 'Turkish' and, despite his earlier refusal, the *una corda*.

Provenance
1993 Sotheby's, 18th November Lot 170. Unsold.
1998 Purchased by private treaty through Sotheby's.

TECHNICAL DATA

Date	c. 1815
Nameboard Inscription	
	Anton Walter u. Sohn
	in Wien
Yoke extension	Oval wax seal initials 'A C' over clasped hands.
Compass	6 Octaves, F_1-f^4.
	Ivory naturals with bone fronts. Ebony capped sharps.
3-Octave-span	479
Stringing	Trichord throughout. Undivided bridge.

	F_1	c^2	f^4
Scaling	1739	281	54?
Strike-point	140	37	15?
Gauges (1997)	1.12	0.56	0.55

C. Barda, London

22.1 Grand pianoforte by Anton Walter and Son, c.1815.

Action	Viennese. Overdampers throughout.
Stops	4 Pedals:
	Keyboard shift
	Bassoon
	Moderator
	Dampers.
Case	Hungarian ash veneered on pine and oak. Length 2184. Width 1139. Depth 260.
Restorations	Awaiting restoration.

23. GRAND PIANOFORTE

by John Broadwood and Sons, London, 1816.
Autographed by J.B. Cramer.

Acquired by The Cobbe Collection Trust with a substantial grant from The Broadwood Trust and funds donated by Alec Cobbe.

This instrument is virtually identical to that chosen by Thomas Broadwood (younger son of John Broadwood) as a gift for Beethoven in 1817. Broadwood had visited Beethoven in the preceding year and decided to make the gesture as a mark of respect to the great man. He was particularly anxious that it should not be publicised lest the gift should appear to be publicity-seeking. On expressing his intention in a letter to Beethoven the composer replied:

My very dear friend Broadwood
I have never felt a greater pleasure than your honour's intimation of the arrival of this piano, with which you are honouring me as a present. I shall look upon it as an altar upon which I shall place the most beautiful offerings of my spirit to the divine Apollo. As soon as I receive your excellent instrument, I shall immediately send to you the fruits of the first moment of inspiration I spend at it, as a souvenir for you from me, my very dear B; and I hope that they will be worthy of your instrument.
    My dear Sir, accept my warmest consideration, from your friend and humble servant,
    Louis van Beethoven.   Vienna 7 February 1818

Broadwood enlisted the help of five pianists in choosing the particular instrument he would give to Beethoven; they included both a former pupil and a friend of the composer, Ferdinand Ries and John Baptist Cramer who was also a fellow composer and virtuoso. The pianists were invited to associate with the gift by signing the instrument which survives in Budapest, a gift to the Hungarian National Museum from Franz Liszt.

English pianofortes were a rarity in Vienna, as indeed were Viennese instruments in London. This is not surprising when one considers that Broadwood's gift had to be shipped to Trieste and then carried overland 200 miles to Vienna. Beethoven was immensely pleased and flattered by this token of international recognition. He was very careful about whom he allowed to touch the piano and showed it proudly to visitors right to the end of his life.

This instrument has a scarcely less colourful history.

23.1 Grand pianoforte by John Broadwood, 1816, autographed by J.B. Cramer.

After being used by Cramer in two evening performances in London with the violinist Vaccari it was shipped at the expense of Cramer's patron the Marquess of Douglas, later 10th Duke of Hamilton, to Florence, addressed to 'His Majesty's Plenipotentiary Ambassador to the Grand Duke of Tuscany, Lord Burghersh'. Cramer was travelling that year and may have performed on it in Florence. Lord Douglas was also living in Italy and is reputed to have been having an affair with Napoleon's sister, Pauline Borghese. Lord Burghersh went on to found The Royal Academy of Music. The instrument descended eventually in the Ryder family, Earls of Harrowby and Viscounts Sandon. It may have come to them in 1897 when the sister of the 13th Duke of Hamilton married Captain Cyril John Ryder, a great grandson of the 1st Viscount Sandon and Earl of Harrowby.

Provenance
The Broadwood ledger entries for this instrument are as follows:
'1816 1st May -Vaccari - Taking 6 Octave GP No 6838 on hire to Mr Vaccari, Argyle Rooms.
Kinsley and Grey'
'1816 2 May - Vaccari - Bringing 6 Octave GP No 6838 from Mr Vaccari, Argyle Rooms. Hire since.   Thurlow and Figg'
'1816 8 May - Burgoyne- Taking 6 Octave GP No 6838 on hire to Lady Burgoyne, 42 Hill St, Berkley [sic] Sq.   Farmer and Figg'
'1816 2 July - Burgoyne- Bringing 6 Octave GP No 6838 from Lady Burgoyne, Berkley Sq. Hire since.   Millett and Mich'
'1816 7 August - Douglas - A 6 Octave GP No 6838 Cover and Case per J B Cramer, The Marquis of Douglas, Grosvenor Place, addressed The Lord Burghersh, Plenipotentiary and Envoy Extraordinary at the Court of Tuscany from His Britannic Majesty, care of Messrs Donat Orsi and Co., Leghorn, delivered at Farlows to be shipped on the Thomas Wm Wright Per Leghorn paid duty entry etc. 29s. Insurance £3 8s. Kinsley.'
The Dukes of Hamilton
Viscount Sandon
Purchased by David Winston at Christie's, London November 1990

Bought from him by Ian Pleeth
1997 Purchased from Ian Pleeth by The Cobbe Collection Trust.

TECHNICAL DATA

Date	1816
Serial Number	6838
Nameboard Inscription	

John Broadwood and Sons
Makers to His Majesty and the Princesses
Great Pulteney Street, Golden Square
LONDON

Wrestplank Inscription	

Signature of J B Cramer

Label on Baseboard	

Fowler's Depositories, Evesham.
Inscribed in pencil *Lord Sandon.*

Compass	6 Octaves, C_1-c^4. Ivory naturals. Ebony sharps.
3-Octave-span	488.
Stringing	Trichord throughout. Bridge divided at $G^\#$/A.

Scaling	C_1	c^2	c^4
Scaling	1922	268	74
Strike-point	166	21	8
Gauges	1.0	0.6	0.56

Action	English Grand - with backchecks. Overdampers to $d^{3\#}$.
Stops	2 Pedals and 1 Handstop:
	Keyboard shift pedal with *una-corda* handstop.
	Dampers - divided pedal.
Case	Mahogany veneered on oak. Length 2434. Width 1135. Depth 294.
Restorations	Restored by D Winston in 1996.

24. SQUARE PIANOFORTE
by Erard Frères, Paris, 1818.

This instrument incorporates an action introduced by Sébastian Erard into his square pianos in 1799 and which was employed largely unchanged for more than two decades. The size of the instruments naturally increased during these years, and Southwell's system has been used in this instrument to include the 'additional' notes in the treble (see No. 17). As with Marie Antoinette's pianoforte (see No. 12), the construction and action are based entirely on English square pianos. In addition to the normal English sustaining and buff stops, Erard, keeping his eye on Viennese developments, introduced a moderator and bassoon, which resulted in four pedals.

As well as possessing an indefatigable genius for mechanics, Erard was always a canny publicist. Haydn, Beethoven and Napoleon all received timely gifts of his pianos. Having recognised the emerging genius of the young Franz Liszt he ensured that his own young nephew, Pierre, partner and heir to the firm, was encouraged in a friendship with the composer. A lithograph (below) of the thirteen-year-old Liszt in 1824 seated at an instrument identical to this one, suggests that such a piano was presented to the boy. Liszt and Pierre Erard did indeed remain close friends and Liszt played Erard's instruments until the advent of the huge Steinway instruments of the 1860s (see No. 35).

Provenance
Purchased from Ian Pleeth by Alec Cobbe. 1997 Given to The Cobbe Collection Trust.

24.1 Franz Liszt seated at a similar instrument (reversed in Lithography).

24.2 Square pianoforte by Erard, 1818.

24.3 Detail of nameboard.

TECHNICAL DATA

Date	1818
Nameboard Inscription	Erard Frères
	Facteurs de Forté-Piano & Harpes du Roi,
	de ses menus plaisirs,
	& de la Cour Impériale de Russie.
	Rue du Mail N° 13 & 21. à Paris 1818.
Soundboard Inscription	
	Erard Frères à Paris 1818.
Compass	5 Octaves and a fifth, F_1-c^4.
	Ivory naturals. Ebony sharps.
3-Octave span	484
Stringing	Bichord throughout.

	F$_1$	c^2	c^4
Scaling	1454	283	64
Strike point	91	25	10
Gauges	Spun	0.48	0.44

Action	Méchanisme à double pilotes.
	(Zumpe's second action).
	Overdampers throughout.
	Overlaid passive soundboard
	(reconstruction)
Stops	4 Pedals
	Bassoon
	Buff
	Dampers
	Moderator
Case	Mahogany veneered mahogany.
	Length 1609. Width 591. Depth 236.
Restorations	Restored to working order in 1978.

25.1 Grand pianoforte by Erard, 1819.

25. GRAND PIANOFORTE
by Erard Frères, Paris, 1819

This magnificent instrument with ornate decoration and nameboard was made by Erard in Paris and supplied to the Duc de Luynes at Dampierre, a château famous for its wall-paintings by Ingres. The nameboard decoration which is signed 'Antoine Rascalon 1818' is realised in a technique known as *verre eglomisé* which involves drawing and painting on the underside of glass and backing the decoration with gold or silver foil. Although the process is named after Jean-Baptiste Glommé (d. 1786) it is much older and probably of Middle Eastern origin. Originally fitted with five pedals and a drum let into the underside, this instrument has an early version of Erard's escapement action. The development of the double escapement was to continue as Erard's life-long preoccupation, and the successful achievement by the end of his life of an action that effectively forms the basis of modern piano actions was his supreme contribution to the instrument's development (see No. 29).

25.2 Detail of Verre Eglomisé decoration.

Provenance
Acquired by M. Stefan Grodée of Amiens from a relative of the Luynes family.
Purchased from M. Grodée by Alec Cobbe.
1997 Given to The Cobbe Collection Trust.

TECHNICAL DATA

Date	1819
Nameboard Inscription	
	Erard Frères
Soundboard Inscription	par Brevet d'Invention No 433
	Erard Freres Facteurs de Fortepiano & Harpes du Roi
	de ses menus plaisirs
	& de la Cour Impériale de Russie
	à Paris 1819.
Inscription underside of top key-lever	
	Pencilled signature "Christtian"
Inscription side of top key-lever, in ink	
	à Dampière anno 1837 mense Julio
	(remainder as yet undecipered).
Compass	6 Octaves, F_1-f^4.
	Ivory naturals. Ebony sharps.
3-Octave-span	488
Stringing	Trichord throughout (Originally).
	Bridge divided $G^\#$/A
Scaling	Not measurable at present.
Action	'Stirrup' escapement with no check.
	Overdampers to f^3.
	Overlaid passive soundboard missing.
Stops	Originally 5 pedals (3 missing):
	Keyboard shift
	Bassoon or buff
	Moderator
	Drum
	Dampers.
Case	Mahogany veneered on oak.
	Length 2050. Width 1096. Depth 269.
Restorations	Awaiting restoration.

26. GRAND PIANOFORTE
by Conrad Graf, Vienna, c. 1819-20.

Graf was one of the supreme makers of pianofortes in Vienna in an era when both Beethoven and Schubert were at the height of their maturity. Both owned instruments by Graf, Schubert's being an early 5-octave model, a present from his father. His instruments

acquired a legendary reputation, and later composers who owned or chose to play them included Chopin, Schumann, Liszt, Brahms and Mahler (see No. 28).

In 1824 Graf made a special instrument for Beethoven with quadruple, instead of the usual triple, stringing. This was a feature of his own devising, never attempted by any other maker, which may have been intended to produce a fuller tone. Beethoven's instrument survives today in his birthplace museum (Beethoven Haus) in Bonn. The instrument in this collection is one of the very few of Graf's instruments remaining today with the quadruple strung system. It was made about four years before Beethoven's and its approximate date can be ascertained, curiously enough, from one of Beethoven's own conversations, the record of which survives in his conversation books. In March 1820 a rival piano-builder, Matthaus Andreas Stein, brother of Nannette Streicher, was trying to persuade Beethoven *not* to have one of Graf's four-stringed pianos. In the conversation, Graf's piano No. 372 is alluded to. The present instrument is No. 365 and must therefore be a little earlier.

Although by this time Viennese pianos were mostly made with the 'English' *una corda* pedal, the original

John Challis

26.1 Grand pianoforte by Conrad Graf, 1819-20.

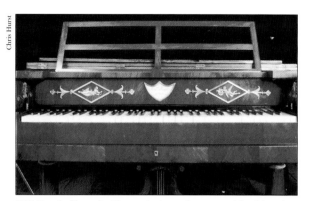

26.2 Detail of keywell with ormolu decoration, unusual for this maker.

26.3 Detail of the name inscription.

Viennese moderator was not abandoned; it was in fact further refined, as in this instrument, where it has two settings, in which the hammers hit the strings through either one or two thicknesses of the moderator cloth. This results in a wide choice of contrasting soft tones being available to the player for which the modern piano has no equivalent, and which are particularly appropriate, for instance, to the music of Schubert.

Provenance
Prior to 1977 found in Styria by Dr Otmar Seeman
1977 Purchased by Alec Cobbe from Dr Seeman.
1997 Given to The Cobbe Collection Trust.

TECHNICAL DATA

Date	c. 1819 -20
Serial Number	365
Nameboard Inscription	
	Conrad Graf
	in Wien
	Wieden 182
Soundboard	OPERA
Inscription	365
	CONR: GRAF
Compass	6 Octaves and a fourth, C_1-f^4.
	Ivory naturals with bone fronts. Ebony-capped sharps.
3-Octave span	478

Hammers	Hammer coverings possibly original.
Stringing	Trichord C_1-$C^\#$. Quadrichord D-f^4.
	Undivided bridge.

	C_1	c^2	f^4
Scaling	1954	270	55
Strike point	178	39	5.5
Gauges	1.42	0.63	0.5

Action	Viennese - with single continuous check.
	Overdampers throughout.
Stops	5 Pedals:
	Keyboard shift (4-2)
	Bassoon
	Moderator 1
	Moderator 2
	Dampers.
Case	Mahogany veneered on laminated oak and pine.
	Length 2415. Width 1234. Depth 316.
Restorations	Restored to working order in 1981.

26.4 Detail of the opus number, clearly showing the quadruple stringing.

John Challis

27.1 Detail of the nameboard © H.M. The Queen 1999.

27. GRAND PIANOFORTE
by Nannette Streicher, Vienna, 1823.
Made for King George IV.

Loaned by H.M. The Queen to The National Trust,
and in the care of The Cobbe Collection Trust.

The Royal Household accounts record that the cost of this instrument was 750 florins inclusive of shipping charges at Trieste and postage freight etc. in London, with 16 florins commission charges in Vienna in all, 766 florins or £86. 4s. 10d. paid to Messrs. Hammersley on May 21st 1824. The pianoforte was moved from Carlton House to Royal Lodge on July 14th 1824. The circumstances surrounding the acquisition by the King of a pianoforte from one of Vienna's leading makers are otherwise unknown. Given the difficulties of transporting instruments between the two cities, and the thriving pianoforte industries in both, the King will have been one of the very few Englishmen to possess a new Viennese pianoforte. After 1810 Streicher was the preferred maker

of Beethoven. In 1823, the year in which the present instrument was made, Beethoven was in correspondence with King George IV asking him to accept the dedication of the pianoforte version of *The Battle Symphony*.

Nannette Stein (see also No. 15) had married Johann Andreas Streicher, and the two had become very friendly with Beethoven, who, according to a number of his letters at various times, preferred her pianofortes to any others and said at one stage that he had been playing her instruments only for a dozen years. It was sufficiently unusual for a woman to be running a business that the Streichers deemed it better that Andreas should conduct all correspondence concerning pianos; therefore when Beethoven was writing about instruments it was always to the husband

- I can't help it, the pianoforte beside the door near your entrance is constantly ringing in my ears – I feel sure I shall be thanked for having chosen this one – so do send it…. (Letter to Andreas Streicher 1810)

Nannette had also taken on the responsibility of hiring

27.2 Grand pianoforte by Nannette Streicher, 1823 © H.M. The Queen 1999.

Beethoven's servants for him and making sure they looked after him properly as well as frequently finding accommodation for him. The longest of his many letters to her is about a missing pair of socks.

It is clear from comparison with other Streicher instruments that the present instrument was a special order and that Nannette must have been aware of its destination. Anglophile as Beethoven was, and given his intimacy with the Streichers and correspondence with the King, it is likely that he took a close interest in the making of this piano and would have been invited to try it before its despatch.

27.3 Detail of the drum mechanism © H.M. The Queen 1999.

27.4 Detail of maker's label, pasted on the soundboard
© H.M. The Queen 1999.

Provenance
1823 Purchased by King George IV from the maker.

TECHNICAL DATA

Date	1823
Serial Number	1756
Nameboard Inscription	

Nannette Streicher née Stein
à Vienne

Soundboard Label

No 1756
Nannette STREICHER *née Stein*
VIENNE 1823

Compass	6 Octaves and a fourth, C_1-f^4. Ivory naturals with bone fronts. Ebony-capped sharps.
3-Octave span	476
Stringing	Bichord C_1-$D_1^{\#}$. Trichord E_1-f^4. Bridge divided at $F/F^{\#}$.

	C_1	c^2	f^4
Scaling	2003	266	51
Strike point	187	32	6.5
Gauges	1.71	0.68	0.52

Action	Viennese - with individual checks. Overdampers throughout. Overlaid passive soundboard (reconstruction).
Stops	6 Pedals, 3 Knee-stops.

Pedals:	Knee-stops:
Keyboard shift	Adds cymbal to pedal 6
Bassoon	Adds bells to pedal 6
Dampers	Adds snare to drum.
Moderator 1	
Moderator 2	
Drum plus other percussion.	

Case	Mahogany veneered on laminated pine. Length 2468. Width 1253. Depth 311.
Restorations	Restored to working order by David Hunt in 1991.

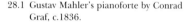

28.1 Gustav Mahler's pianoforte by Conrad Graf, c.1836.

28.2 The maker's plaque and nameboard decoration. See also cover illustration.

28. GRAND PIANOFORTE

by Conrad Graf, Vienna, c. 1836.

Formerly owned by Gustav Mahler.

Despite his successful career, Gustav Mahler was not well-off until his marriage in 1902. His possession of a 'second-hand' piano that in the 1880s would have been distinctly archaic is not as surprising as it might at first seem. Mahler would have been very much aware of the distinction that attached to Graf's instruments in the earlier years of the nineteenth century, and also of their part in the musical lives of Beethoven, Schubert and Schumann. Johannes Brahms, whom he much respected, had taken possession of Schumann's Graf after the latter's death. In 1873 Brahms had presented 'this great relic' to The Society of the Friends of Music in Vienna, of which he was artistic director. Only two years later Mahler entered the Conservatoire of the Society, gaining his diploma in 1878.

Early pianos tend to have a more orchestral sound than modern ones; this applied even in the 1880s and 90s.

Mahler might well have found the tone of the Graf more appealing than instruments of his own time. He was later to persuade Steinway in New York to make a harpsichord for a performance of Bach's Brandenburg Concerto No. 5 rather than use one of their pianos. A most unusual feature of Mahler's instrument may be due to his famously experimental nature. Strips of lead have been inserted under the hammer coverings of notes in the bass register, probably with a view to achieving a more percussive and darker sound.

In 1902, following his marriage into the well-off Schindler family, Mahler was given a new Blüthner piano with a compass of seven octaves and three notes. It is, perhaps, significant that none of the

28.3 Detail of one of the bass hammers, showing the layer of lead introduced amongst the layers of leather.

composer's piano scores exceed the six and a half compass of the Graf. In 1948 when his widow and daughter left Vienna, his daughter Anna presented the Blüthner piano to the Kunsthistorisches Museum. She kept the Graf, which she liked to play herself, and the instrument was acquired in 1993 for the Cobbe Collection from Mahler's grand-daughter, Marina.

Provenance

According to Marina Mahler, her mother Anna and grandmother Alma moved from Vienna to New York after World War II, taking the Graf with them. After Alma's death in 1964, Anna bought a house in Spoleto, Italy, into which she moved taking the Graf piano. It remained there until its acquisition by Alec Cobbe from Marina Mahler in 1993.
1997 Given to the Cobbe Collection Trust.

TECHNICAL DATA

Date	c. 1836
Serial Number	2257
Nameboard Inscription	CONRAD GRAF
	kaiserl:kon:Hof-Fortepianomacher
	WIEN
	nächst der Carls Kirche im Mondschein No 102.
Compass	6 Octaves and a fifth, C_1-g^4.
	Ivory naturals with bone fronts.
	Ebony-capped sharps.
3-Octave-span	478
Stringing	Bichord C_1- E_1. Trichord F_1 -g^4.
	Bridge divided at $G^{\#}$/A.

	C_1	c^2	g^4
Scaling	1887	267	45
Strike-point	169	40	10
Gauges	Spun 1.85	0.72	0.61

Action	Viennese with single continuous check. Overdampers to a^3. Passive soundboard missing.
Stops	4 Pedals originally
	Keyboard shift
	Moderator
	Double Moderator
	Dampers.

Case	Rosewood veneered on laminated pine and oak.
	Length 2434. Width 1250. Depth 326.
Restorations	Awaiting restoration.

29. GRAND PIANOFORTE
by Erard, London, 1837.

The crowning achievement of Sébastian Erard's life-long involvement with the mechanics of piano action was his invention of a double-escapement action which enabled rapid repetition of a note. The purpose was to overcome a serious limitation in previous actions, where the key had to return fully to its starting position before a note could be repeated. With Erard's action the note could be repeated with the key in a semi-depressed position. It took a long time to develop but Sébastian Erard and his nephew Pierre took out the first English patent in 1821. Further work, in which the pianist Moscheles took great interest and on which he gave advice from time to time, took place over the next ten years. This was deemed to have been perfected in 1832, the year after Erard's death, when Mendelssohn was given an instrument probably quite similar to this, which has the perfected action.

Sébastian Erard's work in this field really laid the foundations for the modern piano action. His career had been extraordinarily successful, taking French piano-building from its beginnings right to the eve of the modern era. When he died his family were installed in one of the former Royal residences which was filled with collections of instruments and old master paintings. The latter, numbering more than two hundred and fifty lots, were sold by his nephew in major sales both in Paris and London in 1831.

Provenance
c. 1978 Purchased by Alec Cobbe from a Yorkshire farmer near Goole.
1997 Given to the Cobbe Collection Trust.

29.1 Grand pianoforte by Erard, 1837.

29.2 Detail of name label.

TECHNICAL DATA

Date	1837
Serial Number	15,484
Nameboard Inscription	Erard
	Patent Harp and Piano Forte Maker
	To the Queen.
	No 18 Great Marlborough Street
	London.
Inscription under	London September 9th 1837
Soundboard	No 484. Thos Winington.

Compass	6 Octaves and a fifth, C_1-g^4
	(Originally C_1-f^4).
	Ivory naturals. Ebony sharps.
3-Octave span	496
Stringing	Bichord C_1-E_1. Trichord F_1-g^4. Bridge
	divided at $C^\#$/D.
	Bolted frame.

	C_1	c^2	g^4
Scaling	1790	290	51
Strike point	205	31	6.5
Gauges	Spun2.4	0.75	0.65

Action	Erard patent double escapement and front
	check.
	Underdampers to b^2.
Stops	2 Pedals and 1 Hand-stop:
	Keyboard shift pedal with
	una corda hand-stop
	Dampers
Case	Mahogany veneered on oak.
	Length 2355. Width 1263. Depth 321.
Restorations	Restored by Wingfield pianos before
	acquisition: restrung 1989.

30. GRAND PIANOFORTE
by Erard, London, 1843.
Supplied by the makers to Jane Stirling.
The property of Mr. Alec Cobbe.

According to a maker's inscription at the front of this instrument it was chosen by the composer Julius Benedict on behalf of Jane Stirling (1804-1859) who was then living in Paris, and it was presumably despatched to her there. This was the year she became Chopin's pupil, and it is not inconceivable that his dedication to her in 1843 of his *Nocturnes* Opus 55, was in celebration of the arrival of this very beautiful instrument. Not one to bestow praise lightly, he had a very high opinion of her musical abilities, and wrote to her 'one day you will play very very beautifully'.

David Mees

30.1 Jane Stirling's piano.

They became very close friends. In December 1847 the instrument was probably back in Britain, for Chopin is recorded as arriving for dinner in Paris to try out a further new Erard instrument of Jane Stirling's. In October 1848 the present piano had been sent to Keir House in Scotland, the Stirling family seat then owned by Jane Stirling's cousin, where she brought Chopin to stay during their Scottish tour. Chopin wrote at least two letters from the place describing the *train-de-vie* and how he summoned his strength to play after dinner each evening. The piano either remained at Keir or was later bequeathed by Jane Stirling to her cousins there. The distinguished Chopin historian Jean Jacques Eigeldinger writes of Jane Stirling:

(she) remains famous for her devotion to the person, the works and the memory of Chopin. Many actions inspired by this devotion have established her in the eyes of posterity, to some extent, as the first Chopin 'musicologist'…..we know that this generous Scotswoman bought most of Chopin's estate, also gathering and sorting out many more autographs, letters, papers,drawings and various other objects - which she then either gave to close friends, kept for herself, or forwarded to Chopin's family in Warsaw (such as the last piano he had hired, which she bought from Pleyel after the sealing of the Place Vendôme apartment).

Provenance
1843 purchased by Jane Wilhelmina Stirling.
The Stirlings of Keir.
1981 Keir was sold up and Mrs. Stirling on the advice of her friend Alfred Brendel placed the instrument on loan to Alec Cobbe.
1997 Purchased by Alec Cobbe from Archibald Stirling.

TECHNICAL DATA

Date	1843
Serial Number	713
Nameboard Inscription	Royal Extended Patent

ERARD
Patent Harp and PianoForte Makers
TO HER MAJESTY
To the QUEEN DOWAGER

30.2 Watercolour, view of Keir House, c. 1850.
Courtesy of Archibald Stirling.

To Her Royal Highness THE DUCHESS OF KENT
18, Great Marlborough Street
LONDON

Inscription on Plank
Benedict for Miss Stirling. Pearson.
Inscription under Soundboard
London 1843.

Compass	6 Octaves and a fourth, C_1-f^4.
	Ivory naturals. Ebony sharps.
3-Octave span	497
Stringing	Bichord C_1-E_1. Trichord F_1-f^4. Bridge divided at $C^\#$/D.
	Bolted frame.

	C_1	c^2	f^4
Scaling	1631	286	52
Strike point	210	33	3
Gauges	Spun 2.75	0.82	0.78
Marked gauges		14½	13

Action	Erard patent double escapement with front check.
	Underdampers to b^2.
Stops	2 Pedals and 1 Hand-stop:
	Keyboard shift pedal with *una corda* hand-stop
	Dampers.
Case	Mahogany veneered on oak.
	Length 2222. Width 1275. Depth 326.
Restorations	No work since acquisition.

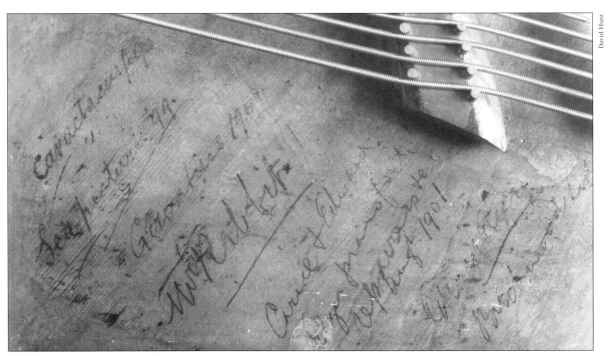

31.1 Elgar's inscriptions on the soundboard.

31. SQUARE PIANOFORTE

by John Broadwood and Sons, London, 1844.
Used, extensively inscribed and signed by
Edward Elgar. *The property of the Royal Academy of*
Music, on permanent loan to the Cobbe Collection Trust.

This instrument was originally delivered by river to
Worcester, where by 1867 it was in the possession of
Edward Elgar's father and uncle who together ran a
business restoring, selling and tuning pianos there.
When Elgar took a small cottage, Birchwood Lodge,
near Malvern, he chose a piano for it from his father's
stock. That he chose this, a square piano then over fifty
years old, has sometimes been attributed to the
smallness of the cottage. However the instrument
occupies more floor space than uprights of the time,

and it is perhaps more likely that Elgar was intrigued,
as Mahler may have been, by the more orchestral
tonalities that the earlier instruments possess.

Whatever the reason, the instrument was Elgar's tool of
composition during a very productive period of his life.
He was sufficiently attached to it, to inscribe on the
soundboard the names of some of the works he composed
upon it. These include *Sea Pictures*, *Caractacus* and *The*

31.2 Keylever recording the restoration by Elgar's father and uncle.

John Challis

31.3 Elgar's piano by John Broadwood, 1844.

Dream of Gerontius: Furthermore, his most famous work, *The Enigma Variations* was both begun, intermittently worked upon and completed at Birchwood using this piano: a momentous output from so small an instrument.

The Enigma Variations was first published in the composer's piano version, and the only recording of the work in this original form has been made on this instrument. It is available at Hatchlands.

Provenance

In the Broadwood ledgers is the following entry:
'1844 23rd July Two square pianos school model Nos. 56664 and 56785 and cases to Mrs Skelton of Worcester. Delivered at Salisbury Arms Cow Lane to go by Crosley's boat. No. 56785 name of Temple written on case.'
1867 Restored by Elgar Bros.
April 1898 Received by Edward Elgar at Birchwood.
1903, when Birchwood was given up, transferred to Pollie, the composer's sister.
1989 Given to The Royal Academy of Music by the Broadwood Trust.
1992 Transferred on permanent loan to The Cobbe Collection Trust.

Elgar's inscriptions on the soundboard are as follows:
'Caractacus …98
Sea Pictures 99
Gerontius 1901
Mr Rabbit!
Carice & Edward Elgar pianoforte repairers & Co Augt 1901
Edward Elgar Birchwood Lodge'

TECHNICAL DATA

Date 1844
Serial Number 56,785
Nameboard Inscription
John Broadwood and Sons
Manufacturers to Her Majesty
Great Pulteney Street, Golden Square,
London
Inscription
On b keylever Repaired by Elgar Bros Worcester 1867

Compass 6 Octaves, F_1-f^4.
Ivory Naturals. Ebony Sharps.
3-Octave span 492.
Stringing 11 Singles F_1-$D^{\#}$. Bichord E-f^4. Stewart Patent.

	F_1	c^2	f^4
Scaling	1366	305	56
Strike point	143	33	10
Gauges	Spun2.5	0.75	0.65
Gauges marked		14	11

Action Single escapement with hopper repetition. No back-check. Overdampers to b^2.
Stops 1 Pedal: Dampers.
Case Mahogany. Length 1705. Width 691. Depth 279.
Restorations Restored by T. Chappell prior to acquisition. Re-restored in 1993.

Restored to playing order with assistance from the respondents to a public appeal.

32. GRAND PIANOFORTE
by Erard, Paris, 1845.
Autographed by Sigismond Thalberg.
Acquired by the Cobbe Collection Trust with funds donated by Alec Cobbe.

Sigismond Thalberg was one of the most celebrated virtuosi of the nineteenth century. Once drawn by the cartoonist Dantan as having ten hands, he was a serious rival to Liszt, and, like him, wrote many elaborate fantasies on opera themes. The instrument is not dissimilar in construction to No. 30, but the Erard workshops, which had operated in tandem both in Paris and London since the 1790s, maintained minor differences of piano design in the respective capitals. Pierre Erard, the nephew and partner of Sébastian, had been put in charge of the London workshops to supervise the final development and patenting of the double escapement action, and probably on account of this Mendelssohn was advised that the London workshops would be preferable for the repairs deemed necessary for his much treasured Erard instrument.

32.1 Grand pianoforte by Sebastian Erard, 1845.

32.2 Detail showing Sigismund Thalberg's signature on the wrest plank.

Provenance

c. 1994 purchased privately in the Channel Islands by Ian Pleeth.
1997 Purchased from Ian Pleeth by The Cobbe Collection Trust.

TECHNICAL DATA

Date	1845
Serial Number	16,994
Nameboard Inscription	

Erard
Par Brevet Paris

Wrestplank Inscription

S Thalberg

Soundboard Inscription

Par Brevet d'Invention
Erard à Paris

Compass — 6 Octaves and a fifth, C_1-g^4. Ivory naturals. Ebony sharps.

3-Octave-span — 494

Stringing — Bichord C_1-E_1. Trichord F_1-g^4. Bridge divided at $C^\#$/D. Bolted frame.

	C_1	c^2	g^4
Scaling	1780	303	47
Strike-point	210	35	4
Gauges	Spun3.2	0.8	0.66
Gauges Marked		15	12½

Action — Erard patent double escapement with front check. Underdampers to b^2. Overlaid passive soundboard.

Stops — 2 Pedals:
Keyboard shift
Dampers.

Case — Rosewood veneered on laminated oak. Length 2375. Width 1290. Depth 335.

Restorations — Restored to working order in 1998.

33. GRAND PIANOFORTE
by Ignace Pleyel, Paris, c. 1846.

The name of Pleyel has been linked by generations of musicians to that of Fryderyk Chopin, because of the composer's preference for their instruments from his arrival in Paris in 1832 until his death in 1849. The firm was founded in 1807 by Ignace Pleyel (1757-1831) composer and publisher, who in 1772 had been Haydn's pupil and lodger. The firm achieved early success by quickly adapting and improving the best features of English piano making. In 1815 Ignace was joined in the firm by his son Camille who was later to become a close friend of Chopin and of whom the composer was heard to say:

There is only one man left today who knows how to play Mozart; it is Pleyel, and when he is willing to play a four-hand sonata with me, I take a lesson.

The action of these second generation Pleyel instruments which appealed so much to Chopin, unlike those of Erard, contained no significant improvements over that employed by Broadwood thirty years previously. Chopin, however, appears to have liked the difficulties that the outmoded action presented. He once said that Erard's instruments, which had a greatly improved action, were 'dangerous', because they sounded so beautiful that one did not realise how badly one was playing. He did nonetheless play Erards on occasions –

When I am indisposed, I play on one of Erard's pianos, and there I easily find a ready made tone. But when I feel in the right mood and strong enough to find my own tone for myself, I must have one of Pleyel's pianos.

Pleyel and Broadwood were on friendly terms and the scarcity of Pleyel instruments in England, and that of Broadwoods in France, suggests that they may have had an understanding by which they desisted from encroaching upon each other's markets. Both makers had to contend at home with the ubiquitous Erard, and

33.1 Grand pianoforte by Ignace Pleyel.

33.2 Detail of name label.

a sympathetic letter from Pleyel to Broadwood written in 1838 fumes about Erard's publicity seeking.

Chopin's last Pleyel piano of 1847, No. 14810, is virtually identical to this instrument. It was purchased by Jane Stirling from Pleyel immediately after Chopin's death and sent as a gift to his family in Warsaw, where it survives in the museum of the Fryderyk Chopin Society.

Provenance
Acquired by Ian Pleeth at auction in East Anglia in the late 1970's.
1988 Purchased from Ian Pleeth by Alec Cobbe.
1997 Given to The Cobbe Collection Trust.

TECHNICAL DATA

Date	c. 1846
Serial Number	13,819
Nameboard Inscription	
	Médailles d'Or 1827, 1834, 1839, et 1844
	Ignace Pleyel & Comp^{ie}
	Facteurs de Pianos
	No 20 Rue Rochechouart Paris.
Compass	6 Octaves and a sixth, C_1-a^4.
	Ivory naturals. Ebony sharps.
3-Octave span	490
Stringing	Bichord C_1-E. Trichord F-a^4. Bridge divided at E/F.
	Bolted frame.

	C_1	c^2	a^4
Scaling	1486	296	44
Strike point	187	41	4.5
Gauges	Spun 2.84	0.84	0.75

Action	Single escapement. (English Grand action).
	Overdampers to d^3 (reconstructions).
	Overlaid passive soundboard.
Stops	2 Pedals.
	Keyboard shift
	Dampers.
Case	Rosewood veneered on laminated oak.
	Length 2037. Width 1276. Depth 311.
Restorations	Awaiting restoration.

34. GRAND PIANOFORTE
by John Broadwood and Sons, London, 1847.
Chosen by Fryderyk Chopin for each of his English recitals.
The property of The Royal Academy of Music, on permanent loan to The Cobbe Collection Trust.

When revolution broke out in Paris in 1848, many of Chopin's acquaintance were implicated. For himself, he judged it timely to accede to Jane Stirling's suggestion of an extended stay in England and Scotland. It was not his first visit to London, as he had travelled there incognito with Camille Pleyel in 1836. On this occasion Pleyel, mindful of the possible attentions of Erard, recommended Chopin to seek his instruments from Broadwood, and the composer accordingly chose three; one to be shipped to Scotland, one for his lodgings, and this one, No. 17047, for his public performances. The occasion was witnessed and documented by one of the clerks of the firm, A.J. Hipkins, who tuned for Chopin during his stay in England, and was later to become a distinguished historian of the pianoforte. Henry Fowler Broadwood's attention went beyond

34.1 Chopin's piano by John Broadwood, 1847.

34.2 Detail of name label.

34.3 Brass plaque affixed to the piano.

looking after Chopin's pianos. When the maestro complained of not having slept well, the firm promptly sent two new mattresses to his lodgings, and for the train journey to Scotland, they booked him two seats so that he would have plenty of space.

Chopin gave at least four recitals in England, one at a dazzling reception at Stafford House (now Lancaster House) given by the Duchess of Sutherland with Queen Victoria as principal guest. Another was given in the St. James's Square residence of The Earl of Falmouth (grandson of Admiral Boscawen, the builder of

Hatchlands). His last was at a Polish Ball given at Guildhall after his return from Scotland. In each one of these the present instrument was used. For some two weeks prior to the Guildhall recital it was in Chopin's rooms in St. James's Place (the house is identified by a blue plaque).

Provenance
June 1847 taken in from factory.
'On Hire' from Broadwoods without charge to Chopin for all his English recitals in 1848.
May 10th 1848 possibly in Chopin's rooms at 48 Dover Street.
November 3rd 1848 moved into Chopin's rooms in St.

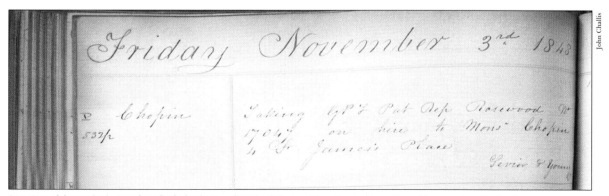

34.4 One of the entries in Broadwood's daybooks recording the delivery of the piano to his rooms on his return from Scotland.

James's Place.

By 1885 sold by Broadwoods to F.H. Appach Esq., Hungerford.

1885 Borrowed from Mr. Appach by Broadwoods for International Inventions Exhibition, London.

1900 Taken by Broadwoods in part exchange for a new piano supplied to Mrs. Appach. A credit of £20 was allowed against the cost of the new instrument - 'This grand 17047 to be reserved, not sold. Chopin played upon it at his Recitals.'

1921 Lent as one of 'fifteen old instruments' to Rushworth and Dreaper, Liverpool.

1922 Lent as one of 'sixteen old instruments' to Harrods.

1989 Given to The Royal Academy of Music by the Broadwood Trust.

1992 Transferred on permanent loan to the Cobbe Collection Trust.

TECHNICAL DATA

Date	1847
Serial Number	17,047
Nameboard Inscription	Patent
	Repetition Grand Pianoforte
	John Broadwood and Sons
	Manufacturers to Her Majesty
	33 Great Pulteney Street, Golden Square,
	London
Lid Plaque	THIS GRAND PIANOFORTE
	WAS USED BY
	FREDERIC CHOPIN
	AT HIS RECITALS IN LONDON
	IN 1848
Inscription under	17045 Maclean
Soundboard	17047
Compass	6 Octaves and a fifth, C_1-g^4.
	Ivory naturals. Ebony Sharps.
3-Octave span	493
Stringing	Bichord C_1-$F_1^{\#}$. Trichord G_1-g^4. Bridge divided at $C^{\#}$/D.
	Stewart Patent. Bolted frame.

	C_1	c^2	g^4
Scaling	1768	297	52
Strike point	188	36	5
Gauges	Spun2.75	0.85	0.75

Action	Broadwood "repetition". Overdampers to b^2.
Stops	2 Pedals:
	Keyboard shift
	Dampers.
Case	Rosewood veneered on laminated oak.
	Length 2468. Width 1258. Depth 334.
Restorations	Work by T. Chappell before acquisition.
	Structure repaired and restrung 1995.

Restored to playing order with grants from Donald Kahn, The Chopin Society, London and respondents to a public appeal.

35. GRAND PIANOFORTE
by Steinway, New York, c. 1864.

After Erard's double escapement, the next really significant development towards the modern piano took place in America with the invention of the cast iron frame. Members made from iron had been bolted

35.1 Grand pianoforte by Steinway, c.1864.

Chris Hurst

35.2 Detail of nameboard.

into the frames of pianos in ever increasing quantities since the beginning of the nineteenth century, as the structure of the instrument needed to withstand greater tensions. The advantage of a cast frame over one with components bolted together was a very much greater strength which enabled higher gauge strings to be used. Steinway was not the inventor of this, but made a further innovation by casting frames that significantly increased the length of the bass strings by running them diagonally over the other strings, leading to the term 'overstrung'. The result was a piano with a markedly greater sonority. The first overstrung concert grand pianoforte was patented by Steinway in 1859. This instrument, made some five years later, is virtually the 1859 model, apart from some minor improvements in the action parts.

Steinway had registered sixteen substantial patents by 1872. Wagner wrote to them eulogising their instruments and Liszt 'changed' to Steinway in 1882, by which time they had acquired a definite pre-eminence over the masters of the mid-nineteenth century, Erard, Pleyel and Broadwood.

Provenance
c. 1978 Acquired by Alec Cobbe from Michael Colt, Bethersden Kent.
1997 Given to The Cobbe Collection Trust.

TECHNICAL DATA

Date	c. 1864
Serial Number	10,654
Nameboard Inscription	
	Steinway and Sons (Later transfer)
	Patent Grand
	New York and Hamburg (Sic)
Compass	7 Octaves, A_2-a^4.
	Ivory substitute. Ebony sharps
	(Replacements).
3-Octave span	497
Stringing	8 Singles A_2-E_1. Bichord F_1-$C^\#$. Trichord D-a^4.
	Overstrung at $C^\#$/D. Cast frame.

	A_2	c^2	a^4
Scaling	1948	306	47
Strike point	220	35	6
Gauges	Spun 4.6	0.96	0.82
Gauges marked		16½	13

Action	Double escapement with backcheck. Overdampers to c^3.
Stops	2 Pedals: Keyboard shift / Dampers.
Case	Rosewood veneered on laminated maple. Length 2559. Width 1387. Depth 345.
Restorations	No major restoration work since acquisition.

36. UPRIGHT PIANO
by Carlo Ducci, Florence, c. 1880
Inscribed and autographed by Franz Liszt
The gift of Dr Vernon Harrison

Little is known of Ducci's piano-making activities, though he is believed to have possessed a showroom in the Via Roma, Florence. The action of this instrument was imported ready-assembled from Schwander in Paris and it is stamped with the records of Schwander's awards in Paris, 1867 and in Vienna, 1873, the latter giving a *terminus ante quem* for the manufacture of the instrument. No other pianofortes by the maker are presently recorded. Carlo Ducci was active as a composer publishing piano pieces and songs in Milan and London.

This instrument, stamped No 1, was inscribed on its wrest-plank by Franz Liszt *Excellent Pianino/ Un meilleur modele F. Liszt.* Mounted on the front of the instrument is a photographic copy of an undated letter from the composer to Carlo Ducci.

36.1 Upright pianoforte by Carlo Ducci.

36.2 Franz Liszt's inscription on the workplank of the pianoforte by Carlo Ducci.

Monsieur Carlo Ducci, Florence
Monsieur
Vous avez eu l'obligeance de me prêter un pianino de votre nouvelle fabrique de Florence. Il est de tout point excellent et reccomandable. On prend plaisir à le toucheret à l'entendre car son clavier souple et sa sonorité harmonieuse charment.

En souhaitant à vos instruments tous les prospères succès qu'ils méritent, je vous prie, monsieur, d'agréer mes sincères compliments avec l'assurance de mes sentiments très distingués.

F. Lizst

[Sir
You had the kindness to lend me a pianino from your new workshop in Florence. It is excellent in every respect and to be recommended. One takes pleasure in playing it because of its supple action and its harmonious sonority is entrancing. Wishing for your instruments all the success they merit, I beg you, Sir, to accept my sincere compliments etc etc.
F Liszt]

In the small corpus of surviving composer instruments this possesses an unusual level of documentation. It was clearly loaned to Liszt during a sojourn in Italy where the sort of instruments he was used to may have been hard to find. It is noteworthy that a modest, domestic piano by a now obscure maker, was not beneath the notice of a musician of Liszt's great stature, and could provide for his musical requirements.

TECHNICAL DATA

Date	1873-1886
Serial Number	1
Nameboard Inscription	Carlo Ducci
Wrest-plank Inscription	Excellent.......... un meilleur modèle F Liszt
Action Stamp	FABRIQUES DE MECHANIQUES POUR PIANOS JEAN SCHWANDER &HERRBURGER

16 Rue de l'Evangile
PARIS

PARIS	VIENNE
1re	1re
CLASSE	CLASSE
1867	1873
Ex[n] Univ[le]	Ex[n] Univ[le]

Stamp under Keybed	FRAT- REALI FIRENZE

	A_2	c^2	a^4

Compass	7 Octaves A_2 - a^4
	Ivory naturals. Ebony sharps.
3-Octave span	485
Stringing	13 Singles A_2 - A_1. Bichord $A_1{}^{\#}$ - c.
	Trichord $c^{\#}$ - a^4

	A_2	c^2	a^4
Scaling	980	295	48
Gauges	Spun 6	0.86	0.68

Action	Schwander tape-check.
	Underdampers to $c^{3\#}$.
Stops	2 Pedals
	Una corda by action shift
	Dampers.
Case	Ebonised Rosewood
	Length 1275. Height 1150. Depth 560.
Restorations	Not in working order when acquired.

37. GRAND PIANOFORTE
by Pleyel Wolff & Co., Paris, c. 1889.

After the death of Camille Pleyel in 1855, the firm was run by his son-in-law August Wolff until his death in 1887, when his son-in-law Gustav Lyon assumed control. The French musical establishment resisted the 'Steinway revolution' longer than almost any other. Pupils were taught at the Conservatoire, and concerts were given virtually exclusively, on the national products - pianos by Erard or Pleyel - right up to the 1930s. Consequently, the clear, glassy sound of this instrument is particularly appropriate for the music of Debussy and Ravel. The company commissioned music from Debussy. The firm eventually merged with the successor to Erard in 1961. The instrument, including its strings and cloth coverings, survives in a fine original state.

Provenance
c.1981 Acquired by Alec Cobbe from D. Adcock, Suffolk.
1997 Given to The Cobbe Collection Trust.

John Challis

36.1 Grand pianoforte by Pleyel, c.1889.

TECHNICAL DATA

Date	c. 1889
Serial Number	81,135
Nameboard Inscription	PLEYEL
Dealer's Inscription	G. S. BOSWORTH
	12 Highfield St, LEICESTER
Lid Inscription	Pleyel Wolff and Cie
Plank Stamp	IB & Co
	London
	No 1111
Compass	7 Octaves and a third, A_2- c^5.
	Ivory naturals. Ebony sharps.
3-Octave span	492
Hammers	Hammer coverings probably original.
Stringing	6 Singles A_2-D_1. Bichord $D_1{}^{\#}$-$C^{\#}$. Trichord D-c^5.
	Overstrung at E/F. Bolted frame.

	A_2	c^2	c^5
Scaling	1933	353	51
Strike point	237	38	5
Gauges	Spun4.6	0.92	0.77

Action	Pleyel patent repetition with backcheck. Overdampers to $c^{3\#}$.
Stops	2 Pedals:
	Keyboard shift
	Dampers.
Case	Rosewood veneered on laminated oak. Length 2548. Width 1397. Depth 324.
Restorations	No major restoration since acquisition.

38. ORGAN
by J.W. Walker & Sons Ltd, London, 1903.

The property of the National Trust.

This instrument was commissioned in 1903 by Lord Rendel from the well-established firm of organ-makers, which was founded by Joseph William Walker in 1820, and established c. 1828 in Museum Street in London near the British Museum. Walker began by making barrel-organs as well as church instruments. His son John James Walker continued the firm after his father's death in 1870 and was responsible for a large number of famous organs. An early surviving example of a Walker organ is at Romsey Abbey, Hampshire and others of later manufacture are at St. Margaret's Westminster, York Minster and Bristol, Liverpool Metropolitan and Blackburn Cathedrals.

The firm continues in practice today and its archives record that the Hatchlands organ was built, exclusive of the case, at a cost of £1000. The handsome and elaborate case was designed by the architect of the room, Reginald Blomfield and carved by Mr. Aumonier who was responsible for all the other ornamental carving in the room. This must have been completed by February 1904, when the Walker archives record the order from Blomfield for the front pipes to be gilded at

a cost of £12. 10s. 0d. The archives also reveal that the mahogany bench was built by Walkers to Blomfield's design costing £8. 10s. 0d in 1905.

Lord Rendel's grandson H.A. Goodhart Rendel, distinguished architect and inheritor of Hatchlands, described the resulting ensemble as ' such as might have been designed by Wren' with its wall-panelling 'interrupted by large, rich, swags of mixed greengrocery beautifully carved by the late Mr. Aumonier in the manner of Grinling Gibbons'.

David Mees

37.1 The organ by J.W. Walker & Sons Ltd.

Aumonier also made 'the tremendous carved organ case... that effectually prevents most of the sound of a large chamber organ from getting out of the instrument into the room'.

Provenance
1903 Commissioned by Lord Rendel and erected in the present location.
1904 Case completed.

TECHNICAL DATA

Date	1904
Nameboard Inscription	By Royal Warrent to H.M. the King
	J. W. Walker & Sons
	London. 1904.
Compass	4 Octaves and a sixth. C_1-a^2. Three manual.
	Pedal board 2 Octaves and a fourth. C_2-f^1
3-Octave-span	491
Action	Mechanical/pneumatic

Registration

Great		Choir	
Open Diapason	8'	Gamba	8'
Open Diapason small	8'	Dulciana	8'
Wald Flute	8'	Lieblich Gedackt	8'
Principal	4'	Suabe Flute	4'
Fifteenth	2'		

Swell			
Lieblich Bourdon	16'	Tremulant	
Open Diapason	8'	Sw Octave	
Echo Gamba	8'	Sw sub-octave	
Stopped Diapason	8'	Sw Unison off	
Voix Celeste	8'		
Principal	4'		
Fifteenth	2'		
Horn	8'		
Oboe	8'		

Pedal	
Lieblich Bourdon	16'
Bourdon	16'
Bass Flute	8'

Couplers

Sw to Gt	Sw to Ch	Sw to Ped
Gt to Ped	Ch to Ped	
3 Comp Ped to Sw		3 Comp Ped to Gt
Gt to Ped on and off.		

Wind Supply	'Discus' electric blower.
Case	Designed by Reginald Blomfield (?) and built by M. Aumonier.
Restorations	No major work recently.

The Cobbe Collection Trust

Donald Kahn and Alec Cobbe in the Library at Hatchlands.

The Cobbe Collection Trust was set up in 1997 as a registered charity in England through the generosity of Donald and Jeanne Kahn, to care for and display the outstanding collection of instruments assembled and donated by Alec Cobbe. Once the charity had been formed, The Baroness Thatcher kindly agreed to become its Patron and has generously supported its activities.

Others whose kindness and generosity has vitally supported the work of the organisation include Allen and Overy, The American Friends of The Royal Academy, The Directors of Booz.Allen and Hamilton, The Broadwood Trust, The Chopin Society, Lady Rose Cholmondeley, Country Life, Hugh Dickinson, Lady Henrietta St George, The Duchess of Grafton, Stephen Gray, John Harris, Dr Vernon Harrison, Adam Johnstone, The Manifold Trust, Peter Mimpriss, Guy Monson, The Museums Commission, Curtis Price, The Royal Academy of Music, The Royal Oak Foundation, Dr Beat Sarasin, The Directors of Sarasin Investment Ltd, Sir John Smith, The Directors of Sun Oil Exploration, David Walker, Jeremy Warren.

Performances of music appropriate to the period of some of the instruments have been made on Compact Disc (available in The National Trust's shop or through the Cobbe Foundation at Hatchlands) and a series of recitals is arranged during the season when Hatchlands Park is opened to visitors. Occasionally special events are organised, both public and private, which include tours when instruments are played in the splendid interiors of Hatchlands Park.

The Trustees may be contacted through, and further information regarding recitals and other events may be obtained from Alison Hoskyns of The Cobbe Collection Trust at Hatchlands Park, East Clandon, Surrey GU4 7RT, UK, tel: 01483 211 474, fax: 01483 255922.

Index